Woodworking Bible [5 in 1]:

Master Step-by-Step Techniques to Craft Extraordinary Wood Projects | The Ultimate Guide for Beginners to Embark on a Journey of Crafting with Wood

**By:
Jericho Lea**

© **Copyright 2023 - All rights reserved.**

The content contained within this book may not be reproduced, duplicated, or transmitted without direct written permission from the author or the publisher.

Under no circumstances will any blame or legal responsibility be held against the publisher, or author, for any damages, reparation, or monetary loss due to the information contained within this book. Either directly or indirectly.

Legal Notice:

This book is copyright protected. This book is only for personal use. You cannot amend, distribute, sell, use, quote, or paraphrase any part, or the content within this book, without the author's or publisher's consent.

Disclaimer Notice:

Please note the information contained within this document is for educational and entertainment purposes only. All effort has been executed to present accurate, up-to-date, and reliable, complete information. No warranties of any kind are declared or implied. Readers acknowledge that the author does not render legal, financial, medical, or professional advice. The content within this book has been derived from various sources. Please consult a licensed professional before attempting any techniques outlined in this book.

By reading this document, the reader agrees that under no circumstances is the author responsible for any direct or indirect losses incurred due to the use of the information contained within this document, including, but not limited to, errors, omissions, or inaccuracies.

Table of Contents

Table of Contents 2

Introduction 5

Book 1: Wood Working for beginners 6

   Introduction 6

Chapter One 8

   Wood Working Basics: Safety Equipments 8

Chapter Two 17

   Tips for dust collection 17

Chapter Three 22

   Setting up your workshop 22

Chapter Four 52

   General tips for shop tool maintenance 52

Chapter Five 56

   Measuring marking and layout 56

Chapter Six 59

   The Safety Guides 59

Book 2: Tools 64

   Introduction 64

Chapter One: 65

- Hand Tools......65

Chapter Two 69
- Power Tools......69

Chapter Three 73
- Stationary and Machine Tools......73

Book 3: Techniques 76
- Introduction 76

Chapter One 77
- Preparing Woods 77

Chapter Two 81
- Joinery Techniques 81

Chapter Three 84
- Sanding and Finishing Techniques 84

Chapter Four 88
- Essential woodworking techniques......88

Book 4: Woods 91
- Introduction 91

Chapter One 92
- Woods......92

Chapter Two 94
- Softwoods 94

Chapter Three *96*
Hardwoods 96

Chapter Four *99*
Veneers *99*

Book 5: Projects *102*
Introduction 102

Chapter One..*103*
Home Accessories 103

Chapter Two *106*
Home Furnishings 106

Chapter Three *108*
Outdoor Projects 108

Chapter Four *116*
Workshop Projects...116

Conclusion *127*

Introduction

There are not many techniques in the world of workmanship that are as time-honored and gratifying as woodworking. Since the beginning of time, the process of turning unprocessed wood into something beautiful and valuable has had a special place in the hearts and minds of artisans. This book, "The Woodworker's Guide: Crafting Masterpieces from Timber," will serve as an all-encompassing introduction to the field of woodworking.

Woodworking is not merely a pastime but a process that requires creativity, patience, and precision. This guide is your reliable friend, whether you are a beginner trying to take your first steps in woodworking or an experienced woodworker wishing to develop your art. On the following pages, you will find the information you need to access the enormous potential that this time-honored art form possesses.

Book 1:
Wood Working for beginners

Introduction

We want to take this opportunity to welcome you to the world of woodworking, which is a place where creativity and craftsmanship meet. This book will be your starting point for a trip that will take raw wood and turn it into beautiful and functional objects. These fundamentals will get you started in the correct direction, regardless of whether you are completely new to the field or want to brush up on your skills.

When working with wood, your tools will become your closest partners. Each instrument, from saws to chisels, plays an important part in giving form to the piece of wood you are working on. As you gain experience, you will learn how to measure, cut, and assemble the project components properly.

But technique isn't everything when it comes to woodworking; you also need to have a good grasp of the material you're dealing with. There are many different kinds of wood, each with its distinct personality. Some of them are strong, while others are more fragile. You must select the appropriate type of wood for your project.

As your self-assurance grows, you will experiment with various styles and approaches. Your skill level will advance with the complexity of the designs you take on, from straightforward boxes to elaborate patterns. And let's not forget the gratification that comes along with applying treatments that accentuate the natural beauty of the wood.

Remember that your safety is the most important thing. Always remember to keep your hands, eyes, and e ars covered. Get training in the proper techniques to enjoy your newfound hobby without worrying about hurting yourself.

Woodworking is more than simply a pastime; it's a journey that lasts a lifetime to begin your adventure into the art of woodworking, gather all of your equipment, including your wood, and grab some tools.

Chapter One

Wood Working Basics: Safety Equipments

Woodworking is a rewarding and creative hobby or profession, but it involves working with sharp tools and powerful machinery, which can be inherently dangerous. Ensuring your safety should be a top priority in any woodworking project. To protect yourself from potential hazards, having the proper safety equipment and knowing how to use it effectively is crucial. This book will provide an overview of essential safety equipment in woodworking.

1) Eye protection

One of our most significant possessions is our eyesight; safety glasses are a simple yet invaluable tool for protecting it. These simple eye protection items can prevent serious eye damage in dangerous environments, including construction sites, laboratories, and even at-home workshops. Ours are very frail and easily broken. Even a droplet or splatter of a harmful material can cause them harm. More than 2.5 million eye injuries occur annually in the United States, with the majority occurring in the workplace or when doing home repair tasks, as reported by the American Academy of Ophthalmology.

Here's where protective eyewear comes in handy: They serve as a barrier to protect your eyes from a variety of threats, such as:

Debris in the Air: Debris can easily go airborne if power tools, hammering, or grinding are used. Protecting your eyes with safety eyewear is crucial when working around such fast-moving things.

Submersion in Chemicals: Safety goggles or glasses with sealed sides are essential in chemical laboratories and other workplaces where dangerous liquids could cause injury to the eyes.

Light Pollution: Welding and comparable activities produce bright light that might harm your eyes. Wearing safety glasses with the right lenses will protect your eyes from this radiation.

Hearing Protection

Woodworking is a pleasurable hobby, but it can also cause permanent hearing loss due to the loud noises you'll make. Constant exposure to loud noises like those produced by table saws, routers, and planers can lead to permanent hearing loss. In light of this, it is essential to always wear protective ear muffs when dealing with wood.

Earplugs or earmuffs will be invaluable allies in this fight. These safeguards allow you to enjoy your hobby without endangering your hearing.

Earplugs, whether made of foam or silicone, are unobtrusive, lightweight, and simple to use. They're great for reducing noise while performing intermittent woodworking chores.

On the other hand, earmuffs are tough and cozy. These headphones provide Complete ear protection, making them ideal for long days in the woodshop. Adjustable earplugs are a convenient way to get a custom fit. It's important to keep in mind that most woodworking equipment produces noises that are over 85 dB, the level at which permanent hearing loss can occur. Therefore, you should always use hearing protection when working with noisy equipment. Woodworking is about making a statement with your work, not how hard of hearing you are. When you consistently use hearing protection, you're doing more than just protecting your hearing; you're also setting a good example for your fellow woodworkers.

Respirator or Dust Mask

Taking care of your health is a top priority when dealing with wood. Protect your lungs and your health with the help of respirators and dust masks. Fine dust particles created during woodworking cause long-term health hazards if inhaled. A respirator or dust mask provides a protective barrier by trapping airborne particles. When compared to simple dust masks, respirators provide far more safety. Fine wood dust can be effectively captured by respirators with the right filters. When doing anything that generates a lot of dust, like sanding or cutting, you won't have to worry about dust getting into your lungs thanks to the tight seal. While dust masks offer some protection, they are most effective in low-dust settings. Choose your respiratory protection with comfort and fit in mind. The effectiveness of a mask depends on how well it seals around the mouth and nose. Maintaining optimal filtration performance requires routine replacement of filters or masks, whether you use a respirator or a dust mask. By taking these precautions, you can make sure that woodworking is good for your health and creativity.

Workshop Ventilation

Adequate ventilation in a workshop is an essential element of a woodworking environment, serving the dual purpose of creating a nice ambiance and protecting one's well-being. Woodworking activities have the potential to emit fine particulate matter, odors originating from finishes, and potentially hazardous chemicals. These emissions might give rise to respiratory and health hazards if proper management measures are not implemented. Adequate ventilation encompasses two fundamental principles, namely dust control and air exchange. The implementation of these procedures has the potential to significantly enhance the workshop environment.

The mitigation of dust: Wood dust, a prevalent result of woodworking activities, has the potential to induce respiratory ailments and potentially severe pulmonary disorders. It is recommended to outfit one's workshop with a comprehensive dust collection system comprising a top-tier dust collector and strategically positioned air filtering units. These devices effectively catch suspended particles in the air, improving air quality and promoting long-term health and wellness.

Air Ventilation: Maintain a consistent influx of unpolluted air into your workshop while simultaneously expelling air that has been contaminated. The desired outcome can be achieved by utilizing apertures like windows and doors and mechanical ventilation devices like exhaust fans. Periodically opening windows and doors facilitates cross-ventilation, thereby reducing the accumulation of airborne particles. The prioritization of workshop ventilation encompasses not only the enhancement of comfort but also the preservation of one's health and the optimization of the woodworking experience. Establishing a hygienic and well-ventilated area fosters an atmosphere where creativity and safety can mutually thrive.

Gloves

Gloves serve a vital function in woodworking, providing essential safeguards and facilitating meticulousness in craftsmanship. The selection of appropriate gloves that balance safety and dexterity is crucial, as they offer additional protection against splinters, cuts, and abrasions. Woodworking gloves are available in a range of materials, each specifically designed for particular applications. Heavy-duty leather gloves safeguard against sharp instruments and abrasive wood surfaces, rendering them highly suitable for lumber handling and hand tool utilization. Cut-resistant gloves are purposefully constructed using particular fibers to protect against unintentional cuts while allowing for dexterity in handling delicate tasks.

Nevertheless, it is crucial to use prudence when making the decision to use gloves in conjunction with power tools. The use of gloves that are not properly fitted can result in entanglement with machinery, hence increasing the potential hazard rather than providing enough protection. When engaging in intricate operations that demand accuracy, such as carving or finishing, performing these activities without gloves or any other protective covering on the hands is commonly recommended. This approach is favored in order to preserve the tactile sensitivity necessary for successful execution. In essence, the primary objective of gloves is to optimize safety measures while concurrently ensuring optimal dexterity and control over equipment. Regardless of one's level of expertise in woodworking, incorporating suitable gloves into the workflow can contribute to maintaining both hand safety and proficiency throughout woodworking activities.

Dust Collection System

A dust collection system is a woodworker's best friend when effectively controlling airborne wood particles and debris. It enhances the quality of the air, which in turn protects your health, and it maintains a clean working environment. In most cases, this setup will consist of a vacuum, dust collector, or extractor that is duct- or hose-connected to your various woodworking tools. It acts as a vacuum, drawing in sawdust, chips, and other tiny particles and preventing them from dispersing around your workplace. Maintaining it on a regular basis is essential to ensuring its efficiency. Using a dust collection system makes breathing easier, cleans the workspace, and helps maintain a safer and more productive environment for woodworking.

Apron or Shop Coat

Maintaining a safe working environment requires more than having the correct tools when dealing with wood. The apron or shop coat is an item of safety equipment that is often overlooked despite its critical role. During your creative woodworking pursuits, you should wear these protective clothes so that you may guard yourself from wood chips, dust, stains, and even little spills. A shop coat or apron can act as a barrier between your clothing and the various messes and dangers that might be found in a workshop. They prevent sawdust and paint from settling on your clothing, lowering the likelihood of skin irritation and the frequency with which you need to change your clothes. In addition, they shield you from small splinters and sharp edges that could graze against you while you're working.

8. First Aid Kit

A well-stocked first-aid kit is a must-have for every woodworking enthusiast. Woodworking requires the use of tools and equipment that, while flexible and creative, can also be dangerous. A woodworking-specific first aid kit can make a significant difference in rapidly resolving minor injuries and ensuring a safe working environment.

A woodworker's first aid kit should comprise the following items:

Bandages and Dressings: Adhesive and sterile dressings in various sizes cover cuts, abrasions, and small wounds.

Antiseptic Wipes and Cream: To clean wounds and prevent infection

Tweezers and scissors: used to remove splinters and cut dressings.

Gauze and tape are required for bigger wounds requiring more thorough treatment.

Disposable gloves: Protect yourself and the injured person from potential contamination.

Burn Cream or Gel: Accidental burns can happen near machinery or hot surfaces.

Pain remedies: Over-the-counter pain medicines might relieve minor aches and pains.

Emergency Phone Numbers and Contact Information: Include emergency phone numbers and contact information for easy reference.

CPR Face Shield: In the event of more serious injuries, having a CPR face shield on hand can be critical.

Place the first aid kit in an easily accessible area in your woodworking workshop to prioritize safety. Check and restock supplies on a regular basis to ensure that the kit is always ready to use. Remember that while safety precautions can help prevent mishaps, having a first-aid kit on hand shows your dedication to the safety of yourself and anybody else working with you.

Fire Extinguisher

It's easy to overlook the possible fire hazards associated with woodworking when you're engrossed in the creative world of art. Wood shavings, sawdust, and flammable finishes are inherent components of the woodworking process. In order to safeguard one's workspace, projects, and personal well-being, a fire extinguisher is deemed an essential instrument.

Selecting the appropriate fire extinguisher:

Selecting a Class A fire extinguisher specifically engineered to suppress fires involving wood materials is advisable. Typically, fire extinguishers of this nature employ water or water-based solutions to mitigate the flames by inducing cooling effects and diminishing the temperature of the combusting substance.

The appropriate positioning:

It is advisable to position your fire extinguisher in a conveniently accessible area within your woodshop, ensuring it is situated at a safe distance from any potential sources of fire. It is imperative to ensure that the object is affixed in a stable manner and that all individuals within the designated area are aware of its precise placement.

Routine Maintenance:

It is imperative to conduct frequent inspections of your fire extinguisher to ascertain its optimal functionality. One should do a visual inspection to identify any observable indications of harm, verify that the pressure gauge is within the designated green range, and ascertain that the pin and tamper seal remain undisturbed.

Emergency Preparedness:

Equally important as having a fire extinguisher is knowing how to use it. Familiarize yourself with the operating instructions and conduct regular fire drills to ensure everyone knows what to do in a fire emergency.

In the world of woodworking, a fire extinguisher isn't just a safety accessory; it's your first line of defense against the unexpected. Incorporate it into your workshop setup to ensure your passion for crafting with wood remains both enjoyable and secure.

Training and knowledge

Perhaps the most critical safety equipment is your knowledge and training. Before operating any woodworking tools or machinery, take the time to understand their proper use and safety features. Attend woodworking classes or workshops to learn from experienced woodworkers, and always follow best practices and safety guidelines.

Chapter Two

Tips for dust collection

In the field of woodworking, the term "dust collection" refers to removing and collecting dust and debris produced during operations involving woodworking. Working with wood generates a substantial number of small dust particles and wood chips, both of which can be hazardous to the health of the person doing the woodworking and the cleanliness of the workshop. These concerns are supposed to be addressed by dust collection devices, which successfully capture and confine the dust and debris.

1. Invest in a high-quality dust collector. An efficient dust collection system in your

woodworking shop starts with a good dust collector. Think about the size of your workspace and the kinds of items you use when choosing a dust collector. The dust your tools produce should align with the dust collector's capacity. A device with a larger capacity than required might be purchased to provide effective suction over time, lowering clogging and maintenance needs.

Dust collectors using cyclones are recognized for their effectiveness. They generate a cyclonic airflow that filters out larger airborne particles before they get to the filter. This improves the dust collection process by improving the suction force and extending the filter's lifespan.

2. Strategically Position Your Dust Collector: Your dust collector's positioning is crucial to maximizing its effectiveness. To reduce the length of ductwork required, place it in the center of your workplace. This lessens the possibility of airflow resistance due to lengthy, intricate ducts. To ensure that dust and debris are successfully drawn into the collector, smooth, straight ducts with few bends and curves maintain constant airflow.

Connect All Tools to the Dust Collection System: Attach every machine that produces dust to the system to increase dust collection efficiency. This includes equipment like sanders, routers, planers, and table saws. To avoid dust leaks, ensure every connection is secure and well-sealed. Leaks can impair the air quality at your workstation and reduce the system's performance

Make Use Of Blast Gates: Blast gates are Beneficial Additions To Your Dust Collection System. Each tool connection point has one of these gate-like mechanisms installed. They give you the option to open or close the ducts, allowing you to precisely direct the suction during various operations. Dust collection efficiency is increased overall by concentrating suction exclusively on the current tool because the system isn't trying to draw from numerous sources simultaneously.

Regularly Clean and Maintain the Dust Collector: Proper maintenance is essential to guarantee your dust collector functions at maximum effectiveness. To avoid overcrowding the collecting bag or bin and lowering suction power, empty it frequently. For filter cleaning and replacement, adhere to the manufacturer's instructions. Clogs, reduced airflow, and poor dust collection effectiveness might result from neglecting maintenance.

Consider air filtration systems: A central dust collector can manage bigger dust particles, but small dust particles can still float around in the air. Consider employing air filtration systems with High Efficiency Particulate Air (HEPA) filters to solve this problem. These machines constantly cycle the air, capturing even the smallest particles that would evade initial collection. This extra step elevates the atmosphere in your workshop as a whole.

Fill Cracks and Gaps: Make sure your workshop is well-sealed to stop dust from escaping. Close any cracks and spaces around windows, vents, doors, and other openings. In addition to improving dust collection, proper sealing makes the workspace more comfortable and energy-efficient.

Use Dust Hoods and Shrouds: Many power tools have dust hoods or shrouds built into them that are intended to remove dust right where it is produced. These add-ons are pretty good at minimizing airborne dust. If your tools lack integrated dust collection capabilities, consider retrofitting or making your attachments to catch dust as close to the source as possible.

Wear the Correct Personal Protective Equipment (PPE): PPE is still necessary even when using an effective dust collection system. Always use a dust mask or respirator to safeguard your lungs against tiny particles that might escape collecting. In order to defend against potential flying objects and loud noise, safety goggles, and hearing protection are also essential.

Create a Regular Cleaning Schedule: You can keep your workspace tidy and organized by creating a regular cleaning schedule. Clean surfaces, workbenches, tools, and floors to reduce dust accumulation. In addition to improving air quality, a clean environment lowers the chance of trips, slips, and falls.

Reduce Dust Generation at the Source: Use practices that produce less debris to reduce dust generation. Maintaining sharp blades and bits will produce cleaner cuts and less dust. Use manual tools or other less-dusty techniques wherever possible to replace power tools.

Become knowledgeable about different wood types. Some woods can be harmful to your health if inhaled, and they all produce different levels of dust. Learn as much as you can about the woods you frequently work in. This information will enable you to take the necessary safeguards, such as improving your PPE or modifying the settings on your dust collection equipment.

Encourage Proper Ventilation: A properly ventilated workspace helps to disperse dust and create a pleasant working environment. If the weather permits, think about installing exhaust fans or opening windows and doors. Proper ventilation supports your efforts to capture dust.

Take into account remote controls: Purchasing remote control systems for your air filtration and dust collector equipment increases convenience and promotes regular use. You can effortlessly turn these systems on and off with remote controls without pausing your work or leaving your workspace.

Always Have Emergency Supplies On Hand: Fire extinguishers and fully stocked first aid kits should be readily available in your workplace due to the possible fire risks linked with dust collection systems. Emergency preparedness safeguards both your safety and the security of your workplace.

You may establish a woodworking environment that yields outstanding creations and protects your health and safety through efficient dust collection and management by paying attention to these thorough suggestions.

Chapter Three

Setting up your workshop

Define Your Workshop's Purpose

Before beginning the process of building up the wood workshop, it is important to determine what that workshop's purpose will be. Consider whether you'll use it for professional purposes, as a hobby, or both. The tools and equipment you buy, as well as the structure of your workshop, are both heavily influenced by this step. If you know exactly what you want to accomplish in your woodshop, you can transform it into an area that serves your needs and also serves as a source of creative inspiration. The first step in creating a workshop that helps you achieve your goals and dreams is to determine what those goals and dreams are. This could be anything from creating amazing furniture to honing your woodworking skills.

Create a Workshop Layout

The first thing to do when putting together a workshop for woodworking is to design a layout that is practical. When planning the space, it is important to keep in mind the workflow, safety, and accessibility of the area. The first thing that needs to be done is to make a detailed layout on paper of where everything, including workbenches, storage cabinets, and other pieces of equipment, will be placed. Consider the dimensions of your work area, the sequence in which events occur, and how your work tends to flow naturally. It is best practice to keep tools routinely used together in close proximity to one another in the storage space they occupy. Keep in mind that your safety should always come first; as a result, you should always give yourself plenty of space around each item. Your layout needs to be flexible. As your expertise and interest in woodworking grow, you might find that certain aspects of your setup need to be adjusted. It is essential to have a flexible mindset in order to fulfill the prerequisites of newly developed tools and technology. A well-organized workshop is essential for any woodworking endeavor because it boosts productivity, enhances the enjoyment of working on projects, and encourages a secure working environment. Having a workshop that is well organized is essential for any woodworking endeavor.

Select an Appropriate Location

The success of your woodworking workshop will largely be determined by the location in which you decide to set it up. Try to find a location that provides a good amount of space for your various tools and tasks. It should contain sufficient natural light and ventilation to make the space conducive to productive labor. In addition, it is important to think about things like accessibility, safety, and concerns around noise, particularly if you are in a residential area. Garages, basements, or specialized outbuildings are all popular alternatives to consider when looking for a space for a workshop. There are benefits associated with each option; nevertheless, the most crucial consideration is whether or not the site meets your requirements and enables you to carry out your woodworking projects comfortably and productively. Take your time analyzing the different possibilities for the location of your workshop so that you can make the right decision.

Gather Essential Tools and Equipment

Setting up a wood workshop starts with gathering the necessary tools and equipment. Important considerations include:

Quality Over Quantity: Invest in high-quality tools appropriate for your project's requirements and skill level. Begin with the basics, such as saws, drills, measuring, and hand tools.

Prioritize safety by purchasing safety goggles, ear protection, dust masks, and a first-aid kit. In any workshop, these are non-negotiable.

Power equipment: Purchase power equipment such as a table saw, miter saw, router, and drill press as your tasks become more difficult.

Hand Tools: Chisels, planes, and clamps are essential for precision work and finishing touches.

Workbenches: Invest in solid workbenches with adequate workspace and built-in storage to organize tools.

Dust Collection: A dust collector or shop vacuum is required to keep the workshop clean, safe, and healthy.

Sharpening and Maintenance Tools: Sharpening and maintenance tools can keep your tools in top shape.

Tool Storage: To improve workspace productivity, organize your tools with tool chests, cabinets, or wall-mounted solutions.

Organize Storage and Workbenches

When putting together a practical woodworking space, one of the most important aspects to focus on is the efficient organization of storage and workbenches. Your workflow will run more smoothly as a result of proper storage because all of your tools and materials will be within easy reach. To make the most of the vertical space available and maintain a clutter-free workspace, you might want to think about installing wall-mounted shelves, tool cabinets, and pegboards. Your workshop's workbenches should be considered its beating heart because they provide the groundwork for all your endeavors. Make an investment in solid workbenches that are up to the challenge of the various woodworking jobs. Keeping the leading equipment within easy reach and ensuring sufficient space for a range of different-sized projects will require careful organization of these items. Not only will you be able to increase the flow of work by effectively organizing your storage and workbenches, but you will also be able to enhance safety by decreasing the likelihood of tripping over tools or materials. A wood workshop that is well organized encourages productivity and creativity, which enables you to focus on doing what you enjoy most, which is making beautiful masterpieces out of wood.

Ensure Proper Electrical Setup

A contemporary woodworking shop cannot function properly without an adequate installation of electrical components. It requires contracting the services of an experienced electrician who will evaluate the power requirements of your workplace and install the essential infrastructure. This includes an adequate number of electrical outlets that have been properly positioned throughout the area so that your tools and machinery may be powered. When carrying out this procedure, safety must always come first. Your electrician will make sure that the capacity of the circuits is accurate, that circuit breakers are fitted to avoid overloads, and that ground fault circuit interrupters (GFCIs) are installed to protect against electrical shocks in settings that may be damp.

It is advisable to have separate circuits for the various kinds of tools in order to avoid overloading the circuits and causing the breakers to trip while they are being utilized. Electrical systems that have been correctly installed ensure that everyone is safe and make it possible to have a fluid workflow. You won't have to keep looking for outlets or worry about the power going out. In a nutshell, a productive and risk-free woodworking space is underpinned by an electrical configuration that has been meticulously developed.

Plan for Dust Collection:

Establishing a woodworking sanctuary encompasses more than merely utilizing tools and honing skills; it also encompasses the imperative of upholding a salubrious and secure milieu. One of the critical factors to take into account when establishing a wood workshop is the development of an efficient strategy for dust collection. Woodworking produces a substantial quantity of delicate particulate matter, which can pose health hazards and compromise the general cleanliness of the working environment. This guide outlines smoothly integrating dust collection into a workshop setting.

Health and safety considerations: The generation of dust particles in the context of woodworking activities may give rise to respiratory ailments and probable allergic reactions. Establishing a dust collection system mitigates the inhalation of those particles, ensuring the preservation of one's health and that of other individuals occupying the same environment.

Centralized System: When designing the layout for your workshop, it is advisable to consider the incorporation of a central dust collection system. Strategically position it to effectively cover the tools and work areas that experience the highest levels of usage. One potential approach entails situating the system in close proximity to immobile equipment such as table saws, jointers, and sanders.

Implementation of Source Capture Strategy: Efficiently position collection stations in close proximity to the primary sources of dust creation. One effective approach is to connect hoses or ducts directly to the tools in order to promptly gather debris at the moment of its generation. This measure effectively mitigates the dispersion of dust particles within the workshop environment.

Designing the Ductwork Layout: Develop a strategic plan for the arrangement of ductwork to ensure efficient airflow. It is advisable to refrain from utilizing lengthy and intricate ducts that may impede the effectiveness of suction. Ensure the establishment of an unobstructed and efficient airflow channel to facilitate the transportation of dust particles from tools to the designated collection system.

Sizing and Power: It is imperative to ensure that the dimensions of your dust collection system are suitably proportioned to accommodate the requirements of your workshop. It is advisable to consider the cubic feet per minute (CFM) rating to align it with the requirements of your tools. Sufficient power is essential for preventing obstructions and effectively removing dust particles.

Filtering: Incorporate efficient filtering mechanisms to capture particles prior to their emission into the surrounding atmosphere. A dual filtration system consisting of primary and secondary filters can effectively enhance air quality. HEPA filters have a high level of efficacy when trapping particulate matter of a fine nature.

Routine Maintenance: It is imperative to consistently clean and maintain your dust collection system to ensure its continued efficacy. The presence of obstructed filters or ducts can result in a reduction in performance and a potential compromise of air quality.

Personal Protective Equipment (PPE): Although dust collection systems effectively mitigate the presence of airborne particles, it is advisable to utilize personal protective equipment, such as dust masks, safety glasses, and hearing protection, as an additional measure of protection.

Acoustic Considerations: Certain dust collection devices have the potential to produce audible noise. Select a system that exhibits suitable noise levels, or contemplate using soundproofing methods to uphold a comfortable and tranquil workshop environment. An effectively devised dust collection approach promotes the cleanliness of one's workspace. It enhances the durability of instruments by mitigating the detrimental effects of dust buildup, thereby minimizing wear and tear. To ensure the optimal health, safety, and overall quality of your woodworking endeavors, it is imperative to conscientiously incorporate dust collection mechanisms into your workshop configuration.

Establish Lighting

Setting up the right lights in your wood shop is a crucial step that will significantly impact how quickly, accurately, and generally enjoyably you can work on projects. You can see your work clearly, pick out details, and measure things correctly with the proper lighting. Here's a better look at the most critical parts of setting up your workshop's lighting:

Find a balance between natural and artificial lighting. Use both natural and artificial light sources. Set up your workshop so that light from outside can come in during the day. This saves energy and makes the room feel more relaxed and welcoming. Add artificial lighting to the natural light to eliminate shadows and ensure the room is always bright.

Overhead and Task Lighting: Put up lights in the ceiling that spread light evenly across the desk. Pendant lights and LED panel lights are great options for this. Task lighting that shines on specific work areas, like your workbench, saw table, or lathe, is an excellent way to add to the ceiling lighting. Adjustable work lights with narrow beams let you shine light on specific areas. Think about the color temperature of your light sources and how bright they are. Choose lights with a color temperature of around 5000K (Kelvin). This is close to the color temperature of natural sunshine and will make your eyes less tired. Adjustable lighting systems that let you change the temperature of the light can be beneficial for different jobs.

Avoiding Glare and Shadows: Put lights in smart places to avoid glare and make shadows as small as possible. This is very important when working with tools or small, complicated parts. Angle your lights slightly to cut down on glare from shiny objects and keep your shadow from falling on your work.

Flexible and portable lighting: Use portable lighting for jobs that require you to move around. Clamp-on or sticky lights can be attached to tools or moved around to ensure enough light wherever you work.

Think about safety: Make sure your lighting setup meets all safety standards. Use light sources and bulbs that are right for a workshop to keep things from getting too hot or starting fires. Keep wires organized and covered to keep people from falling over them.

Upgrade and change: As your projects and needs change, you might want to upgrade or change your lighting setup. New technologies and innovations may give you better ways to light your workshop that use less energy and work better.

Work on Safety Measures

Install fire extinguishers, smoke detectors, and first-aid kits.

Mark emergency exits and ensure they're easily accessible.

Implement safety guidelines and provide training for yourself and anyone using the workshop.

Ventilation and Air Quality

The beginning of your adventure into woodworking should begin with you putting together a well-ventilated woodshop with high standards for air quality. Not only are adequate airflow and controlled dust levels crucial for your health, but they are also essential for the longevity of your tools and the precision with which you perform your task. Consider how the flow of air will be affected by the layout of your workshop as you put it up. Workstations should be arranged in such a way as to maximize ventilation while avoiding the creation of "dead zones" that could become breeding grounds for allergens and other airborne pollutants. Because windows and doors can act as natural sources of ventilation, you should arrange your tools and workbenches so that they take advantage of these features to the greatest extent possible.

Putting in Place an Exhaust System:

When removing hazardous airborne particles and preserving air quality, installing an exhaust system that is up to the task is of the utmost importance. Wood particles and fine dust will be produced during the cutting, sanding, and shaping. These will be collected by a dust collection system equipped with the appropriate filters. Ensure that your exhaust system is the right size for your workplace, and give it routine maintenance to ensure it is operating at its full potential.

Employing Devices for the Filtration of Air

In woodworking workplaces, air filtration systems are smart expenditures that should not be overlooked. These machines recirculate and filter the air, removing even the tiniest bits of dust from their surroundings while simultaneously cleaning the atmosphere. Installing strategically located air filtration units within your workshop will ensure that the air is continuously cleaned while you are there.

Positioning of Workstations According to a Strategic Plan:

A consideration of ventilation should go into positioning your workstations, such as saws and sanding areas. Position these stations near windows or other emission sources to facilitate the immediate removal of dust and fumes from the area. This stops them from moving throughout the workshop and settling on your tools and surfaces.

Putting on your protective equipment, also known as PPE:

Although adequate ventilation is of the utmost significance, the need to wear personal protection equipment should not be discounted. Protecting yourself from the potentially hazardous dust and noise caused by woodworking activities can be accomplished by donning a high-quality dust mask, a pair of safety glasses, and hearing protection.

Regular Cleaning of the Workshop:

Keeping the surfaces in your workshop swept and vacuumed regularly will help you keep it clean. This practice helps to manage dust levels and prevents debris from interfering with the performance and precision of your tools. In addition, it helps to manage dust levels.

Taking Charge of the Relative Humidity:

Wood is sensitive to fluctuations in humidity, which might affect the quality of your work if the humidity is not stable. Installing either a dehumidifier or a humidifier will help you maintain humidity levels within the ideal range, reducing the risk of your woodwork being warped or cracked.

Individual Well-Being and Contentment:

Not only is it important to protect your projects, but it's also important to protect your health by maintaining a high level of air quality and ventilation. Poor air quality has been linked to a number of respiratory and allergic conditions. You can make your workshop more pleasant and conducive to productive work by maintaining the air quality.

11. Flooring and Surface Materials

Concrete Flooring: The Rock-Solid Foundation

Concrete is one of the most favored choices for workshop flooring, and it's not without good reason. Its inherent durability and ease of maintenance make it the cornerstone for many wood workshops. Concrete can take the weight of heavy machinery, endure the hustle and bustle of high foot traffic, and still stand firm. Consider applying an epoxy coating to your concrete floor to enhance its performance. This addition fortifies the surface and provides resistance against spills, stains, and the inevitable abrasions of woodworking. The result is a smooth, easy-to-clean canvas that promotes a tidy and safe workspace, allowing your craftsmanship to shine without a cluttered or unsafe environment.

Rubber Flooring: Comfort Underfoot

Imagine spending long hours in your wood workshop, meticulously crafting your masterpieces. Rubber flooring offers an ergonomic solution to combat the fatigue that inevitably accompanies hours of standing. Its cushioned surface provides a layer of comfort, absorbing shock and reducing strain on your feet and joints. Safety is paramount in a woodworking environment where spills and accidents can happen. Rubber flooring, with its slip-resistant properties, ensures you maintain your footing even in the face of unexpected messes. This makes it an excellent choice for a space where comfort and safety are top priorities.

Wood Flooring: Aesthetics Meets Practicality

The allure of wood flooring in a wood workshop is undeniable. It evokes a warm, inviting atmosphere and can help dampen the noise created by woodworking machinery. However, there are critical factors to weigh before committing to wood. While wood is aesthetically pleasing and can enhance the ambiance of your workshop, it is more vulnerable to damage from heavy machinery and the occasional dropped tool. If you embrace wood flooring, choose challenging and dense wood species like oak or maple. Additionally, consider placing protective mats or rugs in high-traffic areas to shield your beautiful wood floor from unnecessary wear and tear.

Vinyl Flooring: Durability with Versatility

For those seeking a balanced approach to durability and cost-effectiveness, vinyl flooring proves to be a wise choice. Resistant to moisture, spills, and stains, vinyl flooring offers ease of cleaning and maintenance. Its versatility extends to aesthetics, with various styles available, including those that convincingly mimic the appearance of wood or tile. This flexibility allows you to create a visually appealing workshop environment without compromising functionality. With vinyl flooring, you can have a workspace that's easy to maintain and suits your design preferences.

Mats and Anti-Fatigue Matting: Comfort and Protection

Irrespective of your chosen flooring material, the inclusion of anti-fatigue mats in crucial work areas is a wise investment. These mats serve as a cushioned haven for your feet, reducing the strain associated with prolonged periods of standing. Furthermore, they act as a protective barrier against the unforgiving impact of dropped tools, ensuring both your comfort and the longevity of your workshop flooring.

Workbench and Table Surfaces: Crafting Durability

The surfaces of your workbenches and tables warrant special attention, as they are the primary stages for your woodworking creations. To withstand the rigors of woodworking tasks, consider materials like laminated particleboard or hardwood plywood for these surfaces. Their durability ensures they endure the pressures of cutting, sanding, and assembling your projects. For added practicality, consider applying a sacrificial top layer to these surfaces. This thin layer, often made of hardboard or MDF (medium-density fiberboard), can be easily replaced when worn or damaged. This approach extends the life of your workbench and tables, allowing them to serve as reliable partners in your woodworking journey for years.

Finishing and Sealing: Preserving Your Workshop's Integrity

Applying appropriate finishing and sealing products is paramount regardless of your select flooring and surface materials. For wood surfaces, such as workbenches and tables, the application of polyurethane or varnish is recommended. These finishes protect against spills and stains while enhancing the wood's natural beauty. When dealing with concrete flooring, sealing is a critical step. This process prevents moisture infiltration and shields the surface from potential chemical damage. By sealing your concrete floor, you ensure its longevity, thereby safeguarding the very foundation upon which your woodworking dreams take shape.

In this in-depth exploration of flooring and surface materials, you've learned that every element in your wood workshop serves a vital role. The choice of materials, whether concrete, rubber, wood, vinyl, or protective mats, should align with your specific needs for durability, comfort, safety, and aesthetics. Your workbenches and tables, the workhorses of your workshop, deserve sturdy surfaces that can endure the test of time, complemented by appropriate finishes and sealants to protect your investments.

As you set up your wood workshop, remember that the flooring and surface materials you choose are practical components and the foundation upon which your woodworking journey is built. By making informed decisions in this realm, you'll create a workspace where creativity and craftsmanship flourish unhindered. Stay tuned for more insights as we continue to build your woodworking expertise from the ground up. Happy woodworking!

12. Stock Up on Materials

Putting together a woodworking shop is like getting ready for a creative adventure. In the same way an artist chooses their canvas and paints with deliberation, a woodworker must carefully compile an extensive collection of materials to create their masterpieces. In this chapter, we'll delve into the essential components that serve as the basis for your woodworking pursuits so that you can build a strong foundation.

Lumber is the lifeblood of the woodworking industry.

Lumber, the fundamental component of woodworking, carries the potential for alteration embedded within its grain. Every kind of wood has its distinct personality, from the dignified air of oak to the sweet enticement of cherry. The selection of the appropriate species of wood is in and of itself an artistic endeavor, with consideration given to aspects such as grain patterns, longevity, and workability. Take into consideration the scope of your projects before making any lumber purchases. Depending on the project, wood must be cut and sourced from various species. The sturdiness of walnut may make it an excellent choice for constructing a sturdy dining table, while the understated beauty of maple may be well suited for a jewelry box. Because of this, it is a good idea to keep a variety of lumber in various sizes to fulfill all of your woodworking ambitions.

Sheet Goods: A Versatile Option with Handcrafted Quality

In your woodshop, sheet goods such as plywood and medium-density fiberboard (MDF) serve as the multipurpose canvas onto which you may create magnificent works of art. You can use plywood, graded according to the number of plies and the quality of the veneer it contains, as the support system for your cabinetry or as a structural miracle in your next project. On the other hand, MDF has a smooth surface that can be painted, making it an excellent choice for projects that place a premium on producing a faultless finish. When you are purchasing sheet goods, you should take into consideration the quality and thickness that is appropriate for the work you have envisioned. Your woodworking expertise will frequently be determined by the foundation you select, and using these materials allows you to showcase your artistry.

The Functional Beauty Hidden in the Details of the Hardware

The woodworking industry is full of unsung heroes in the form of hardware, which includes a wide variety of essential components. Even while screws, nails, hinges, handles, and knobs may look like unimportant features, they play an important part in the assembly process and the final product's functionality. Every component of the physical system is an element that contributes to the overall manifestation of your vision. Consider the variety of tasks you plan to work on in your woodshop so that you can supply it appropriately. Hardware is available in various shapes and sizes, each designed to fulfill a particular need. Investing in a wide collection will allow you to add elements to your works that are both utilitarian and aesthetically pleasing.

The Art of Preserving and Enhancing Beauty Through Finishes and Sealants

Within the realm of woodworking, finishes and sealants serve the purpose of an artist's palette. They not only shield your projects from the wear and tear that comes with the passage of time, but they also accentuate the natural beauty of the things they protect. You can generate feelings through your work using stains, paints, varnishes, and sealants. These are the tools you use. Ensure that you have a wide selection of different finishes in stock to meet the specific requirements of each job. Whether you want to highlight the wood's natural grain or produce a sleek and modern finish, having a spectrum of finishing materials on hand will guarantee that your vision is translated into a successful outcome.

The Adhesives and Glues That Hold Everything Together

When dealing with wood, the durability of your work frequently depends on the soundness of joints that are not visible. The choice of glue can determine the success or failure of a project. Be sure to stock up on adhesives such as wood glue, epoxy, and other varieties adaptable to various substrates and uses. Having the appropriate adhesive on hand is paramount when making solid and long-lasting connections.

Protecting Yourself and Your Craft with the Appropriate Safety Gear

Safety should always be the priority in a woodshop. Your arsenal of protective equipment, including goggles, ear plugs, dust masks, and gloves, protects against the dangers inherently associated with woodworking. By emphasizing safety, you can ensure not only the durability of your product but also your well-being and the well-being of people in the vicinity.

Fundamentals of the Workshop: Instruments for Accuracy and Perfection

When working with wood, precision is of the utmost importance. Sandpaper, measuring instruments (such as tape measures, squares, and rulers), marking tools (pencils, markers, and chalk), and clamps are the unsung heroes that enable you to achieve the accuracy required for your projects. Clamps are the unsung heroes that enable you to achieve the accuracy required for your projects. Be sure to stock up on these necessities, as exact measurements, markings, and assembly require their use.

Keeping the Workshop Organized and Securing the Tools Is Its Backbone.

Your woodworking masterpieces require a well-organized studio to serve as the canvas upon which they are shown. You might consider investing in storage solutions like shelves, cabinets, and tool racks. Not only will this ensure that your materials and tools are easily available, but they will also demonstrate your dedication to the craft. A productive workshop is kept clean and organized.

13. Personalize Your Workshop

Your workshop is more than just a place to do your work; it is also your sanctuary and home for creative endeavors. Customizing it not only improves its functionality but also enables it to serve as an expression of the passion you have for woodworking.

Design and Flow of Operations

Imagine your workshop is a blank canvas just waiting to be painted on by your style. Your first attempt at painting will be the layout. The key is to design a location that satisfies your woodworking requirements and encourages productivity and originality. Think about the dimensions and layout of your workshop. Do you flourish in a large, open floor plan where you can roam freely between workstations, or do you like the intimacy of a small area where everything is kept within arm's reach? Your workflow should be aligned with your layout so that you may move fluidly from one activity to the next. This will make your workflow more efficient. Consider the order in which you do your tasks. Where will you begin working on your projects, and where do you want them completed? How can your tools and workstations be positioned such that you spend as little time as possible moving around? When you customize your workshop, the answers to these questions will become your guiding lights. They will ensure that your woodworking sanctuary is carefully tuned to the exact projects you have in mind, whether those projects require the making of exquisite furniture or detailed woodcarvings.

The illumination of lighting in your workshop is not only something that needs to be done, but it is also an art form. Imagine the brilliance of the natural light that comes in via the huge windows and skylights and how it instantly makes you feel welcome. It illuminates your workspace and improves your spirits as you work on your crafts, which is a win-win. On the other hand, working with wood is not limited to daylight hours. When natural light is sparse, such as in the evenings, overcast days, or during the winter months, invest in LED lighting of a high quality that can be adjusted. These lights simulate the natural spectrum; as a result, they alleviate eye strain and make it possible for you to see every aspect of your projects in exquisite detail. Not only can customizing the lighting in your workshop improve its functioning, but it will also produce an atmosphere in which your enthusiasm for woodworking will flourish.

Ventilation and Collection of Excess Dust

Dealing with wood can generate a lot of dust, and the odors produced by finishes and glues aren't always pleasant. Taking care of your health and maintaining your well-being is an important part of personalizing your workshop. Installing an efficient ventilation system helps remove potentially hazardous particles and guarantees that your air will remain clean. It would help if you considered installing a dust collection system to maintain a clean working environment and save your lungs. Woodworkers are well aware that a tidy workshop leads to increased productivity. Installing an air filtration system in your workshop will allow you to collect even the smallest dust particles, keeping your space clean and ready for the next project you have in mind.

The Selection of Tools

The quality of your craftsmanship is reflected in the tools you use. Your style of woodworking and your level of expertise should be reflected in them. Whether you choose hand tools' accuracy or power tools' speed, you can customize your toolbox to reflect how you prefer to work. Choose high-quality tools that fit your hand well, offer a pleasant overall experience, and are designed for the jobs you enjoy working on. Your selection of tools ought to result from a thoughtful and individualized process to ensure that each tool fulfills a function and adds to the overall quality of your work.

Various Options for Storage

Storage in your workshop is analogous to the backbone of a nicely organized space. Modify it to suit the specific requirements of your tool collection, the materials you use, and the projects you currently have going. Modify the dimensions of the shelves, cabinets, and drawers so that you can make the most of the available space and maintain easy access. A well-kept and well-organized workshop helps you save time and makes the space risk-free by reducing the likelihood of accidents brought on by disorganization. Because every instrument and piece of material in your customized workshop has a specific location, you will have an easier time concentrating on your craft.

Bench: Your workbench is the beating heart of your workshop and the place where your creations are given form and substance. Adjust it to fit your height, style, and how you operate. Consider including built-in vises, clamps, and storage to turn your workspace into a flexible and productive area that meets all your requirements. Because the workbench is where your passion for woodworking takes form, you should make sure that it is designed to provide the necessary support and functionality for the projects you are working on.

Precautionary Measures

Safety is paramount when dealing with wood; your workplace should reflect that. Make it your own by installing safety elements like fire extinguishers, first aid kits, and marked departure routes in case of an emergency. Adjust the fit of your protective equipment (PPE) so that it is comfortable while providing the level of protection required for the activities you will be performing. Not only should your workshop be a haven for your creative expression but also for your physical and mental health. It is necessary to take personalized safety measures to safeguard yourself and the people who share your workspace.

The Zone of Inspiration

Personalization encompasses not only the function of an item but also its aesthetic value. Ensure your workshop has a designated "inspiration zone" or an area encouraging innovative thinking. Install a bulletin board as a piece of decor so that you may pin up ideas for projects and phrases that motivate you. The artwork you choose to hang should reflect the spirit of your woodworking. Exhibit photographs of woodworking greats and completed works to serve as a constant reminder of the limitless potential of your chosen field. The walls of your inspiration zone can serve as a canvas for your creative endeavors, encouraging you to undertake new projects and expand your woodworking horizons.

A Pleasant Environment To Work In

14. Start Small and Expand Gradually

Creating your woodworking shop is analogous to beginning an exciting journey into handiwork and crafting. However, much like the rest of the journey, a great start depends on a well-thought-out plan. This chapter will discuss the benefits of beginning your woodworking workshop on a modest scale and expanding it over time. Adopting this strategy is essential to your success in woodworking, which is analogous to growing a sapling into a strong tree via careful tending.

- Make sure you have a crystal-clear picture of where you want to go with your woodworking career.

Take a moment to think about what you want to accomplish with your woodworking hobby before you rush out to buy tools and supplies. What kinds of projects pique your interest the most? Which type of tool appeals to you more—the accuracy of hand tools or the speed and convenience of power tools? Developing a distinct vision for your future in woodworking is analogous to charting a course; it guides your decision-making and determines your workshop's path.

- Select the Appropriate Location: the Peaceful Retreat That Is Your Workshop

The place you decide to hold your workshop is of the utmost importance. In an ideal world, it would be a private haven where you could indulge in unfettered creative expression without being disturbed. In the beginning phases of your woodworking pursuits, even a little space, such as a corner of your garage or basement, can serve as a humble yet productive ground for your projects. Ensure plenty of natural light, enough ventilation, and easy access to power outlets in this area.

- Make an Investment in Necessary Equipment, Which Serves as the Foundation of Craftsmanship

As you get started in the world of woodworking, you should direct the early purchases you make on fundamental instruments that are in line with your goals. Consider the workbench to be the throbbing heart of your workshop. Build it yourself or buy it, but put functionality and durability at the top of your priorities.

Hand Tools: These are the extensions that artists use. Acquiring fundamental hand tools such as chisels, saws, planes, and precision measuring devices is essential to perform work with high attention to detail.

Safety Equipment: Put your well-being first at all times. Make sure you safeguard your eyes, ears, and respiratory system by investing in a dust mask, safety glasses, and hearing protection.

- Develop your skills through the completion of simple projects, as these provide the best environment for skill development.

The appeal of huge undertakings may be alluring, but the wise thing to do is focus on smaller, more beginner-friendly endeavors when you're just starting. These tasks act as the nutrient-rich soil in which your abilities can take root and grow. Consider the process of making cutting boards, basic shelves, or exquisite picture frames as an early stage in the development of your trade.

- Become Familiar with Effective Workshop Layout: How to Balance Productivity and Safety

Keeping things orderly in the workshop requires a focus on both productivity and safety. Create the arrangement of your workshop with balletic perfection that will allow the tools and workstations to flow together without any interruptions. In order to maintain an environment that is conducive to both creativity and well-being, it is important to give priority to spaciousness for fluid movement and to consider dust collecting methods.

- In time, broaden the scope of your tool collection to accommodate the expanding capacity of your toolbox.

Allow the natural expansion of your tool collection as your woodworking expertise develops and you tackle increasingly tricky jobs. Choose tools that are appropriate for the projects you want to take on in the future. This strategy not only lightens the financial load but also assures that every tool is used in the most productive way possible in your capable hands.

- Make Organization a Habit: Mastering the Art of Tidiness and Productivity

A seasoned craftsman will always have a well-organized workplace. It is one of the telltale signs of their success. To keep your workspace organized and clutter-free, investing in storage solutions such as cabinets, shelves, and tool racks is important. The transformation from unproductive chaos into fruitful creativity is possible.

- Adapt and Improve as Necessary: The Development of Mastery

As you progress, you may realize that particular gear or tools are no longer compatible with your expanding talents and goals. Upgrade strategically. Although purchasing quality tools is an investment, they typically have a longer lifespan and produce superior results, making them valuable companions on your road to becoming a better woodworker.

- Seek Advice and Consider Becoming a Member of a Community, Such as the Fellowship of Woodworkers

The journey of a woodworker is traveled by many. Do not be afraid to seek the advice of woodworkers with years of experience. Consider joining a group or organization specializing in woodworking in your area. These connections not only provide direction but also a wealth of fellowship, feedback, and ideas as well.

- The steadfastness of craftsmanship can be attributed to patience and perseverance

Remember that working with wood is a skill that improves with practice. Develop your capacity for self-control and patience. Embrace the fact that mistakes are the building blocks of your education. Be steadfast in your efforts to hone your skills. Your path from being an amateur woodworker to an expert will demonstrate your commitment and enthusiasm, much like the growth of a tree from a small seedling to a towering oak.

15. Learn and Practice Safety Protocols:

Health and safety should always be your first concern in your woodworking shop. In this chapter, we will discuss a variety of vital safety regulations and principles that will assist you in establishing a risk-free and protected setting for your woodworking endeavors.

Design and Organization of the Working Area

It is essential to give careful consideration to the organization of your workstation before you even begin to use your equipment. Make sure there is appropriate space, adequate lighting, and adequate ventilation. Also, make sure there is enough room to move around. You can maintain a clean and organized work space by allocating designated locations for your equipment, materials, and completed projects. This arrangement not only improves productivity but also reduces the likelihood of unfortunate events happening.

Personal Protective Equipment, or PPE, includes the following

Not wearing the proper personal protective equipment (PPE) is necessary in woodworking. Always protect your eyes by wearing safety glasses or goggles to prevent injury from flying particles. Hearing protection, a dust mask, and gloves should always be worn depending on the activity. Shoes with closed toes and non-slip soles are required at all times to prevent injuries from objects or instruments that may fall.

Concerning the Care and Upkeep of Tools

It is imperative that tools undergo routine maintenance in order to ensure that they can be used in a secure and effective manner. Make sure that your tools are always clean, sharp, and in the correct calibration. Always use the product in accordance with the instructions provided by the manufacturer. Always make sure the power is turned off to the power tool before making any adjustments or changing the blades or bits. In addition, make sure that your cutting tools are always sharp so you don't have to overwork yourself to get them to cut properly.

Prevention of Fires

Working with wood necessitates handling a variety of substances, some of which are highly combustible. In your workshop, make fire extinguishers easily accessible by installing them in strategic positions. Keep your work area clear of combustible liquids and flammable rags, and don't use power equipment while they're close to sources of ignition.

Security in Electrical Systems

It is essential that you manage the electrical connections in your workshop in a safe manner. Plugging one high-powered tool at a time into a given outlet may prevent the circuits from overloading. Before you use any cables, check them for any signs of fraying or damage. If you want to protect yourself from getting shocked by electricity, you should think about investing in ground fault circuit interrupters (GFCIs).

Collecting Dust and Providing Ventilation

Wood dust can harm one's health; therefore, investing in a dust collection system is vital. It preserves the cleanliness of your workshop and keeps the air quality stable. A sufficient amount of ventilation helps remove lingering odors and prevents the accumulation of potentially hazardous airborne particles.

Preparedness for Emergencies

Accidents can still occur even when measures are taken; therefore, preparation is essential. Your workshop should always have a well-stocked first aid kit, and you should be familiar with how to utilize it. Have a well-defined emergency plan that details how to get out of dangerous situations, where to find fire extinguishers, and who to call in an emergency.

Education and Professional Development

Having the appropriate training is essential to working safely. Acquaint yourself with the many pieces of equipment and tools that you will be utilizing. Seek out woodworking workshops near you, or look for online tutorials to learn the appropriate methods and how to be safe while you work. You should never try a task for which you lack the requisite abilities until you have mastered those skills.

16. Maintain and Upgrade Regularly

- Regularly clean and maintain your tools and equipment.

- Consider upgrades and improvements as your skills and needs evolve.

17. Join a Woodworking Community

Find local woodworking groups or join online communities dedicated to the craft in order to receive support, guidance, and ideas. Having ties to the local community can be beneficial in the following ways:

Opportunities for the Exchange of Knowledge and the Acquisition of New Skills

The priceless wealth of information that is freely exchanged among members of any woodworking community is the activity that serves as the community's beating heart. Imagine you are part of a broad group of woodworkers, from eager beginners to virtuosos with decades of experience. In this place, expertise is not hoarded but rather freely given forth. Participate in thought-provoking gatherings, dive into thought-provoking forums, and enlightening workshops. You will unearth a treasure trove of strategies, tips, and tactics that would otherwise take you years to discover in the solitary confines of your workshop if you did not participate in this activity.

Access to Various Resources and Instruments

Establishing your wood workshop typically comes with a heavy price tag, particularly when collecting the arsenal of tools and equipment required to woodworking. Thankfully, groups that focus on woodworking typically provide shared workshop spaces as well as programs that hand out tools. Due to the openhanded nature of this strategy, you will be able to acquire access to a vast collection of tools without having to face the huge financial load of purchasing them all at once. This functionality not only reduces the burden on your finances but also broadens your horizons by enabling you to play with a wide variety of tools, which in turn broadens your understanding of the world.

Boost to One's Creativity and Inspiration

Imagine becoming a member of a dynamic community of woodworkers, where you are regularly exposed to a wide variety of woodworking projects and styles. This exposure is analogous to having a museum full of ideas readily available to you at any given moment. Being able to observe the skill and originality displayed by your fellow woodworkers may be an extremely motivating experience. It has the capacity to reawaken the original creative vision that is uniquely yours. Participate in lively conversations, share and receive ideas, and gain insight from constructive criticism. Within carpentry, a setting that encourages collaboration will help you come up with unique and impressive items that stand out from the crowd.

Enhancement of Capabilities and Safety

The art of woodworking can be extremely satisfying, but it also presents a number of risks. The community of woodworkers has a wealth of knowledge that extends to safety training and guidelines, both of which have the potential to save lives. You will be able to avoid mishaps and injuries by following the advice of experienced woodworkers who have accumulated a wealth of knowledge over the course of their careers and can direct you toward safe working procedures. In addition, you can accelerate your path to woodworking expertise by receiving hands-on instruction and constructive criticism within the context of this welcoming community, an opportunity not available anywhere else.

Building Relationships and Working Together

Networking opportunities and opportunities to work together can flourish in groups devoted to woodworking. You will have the opportunity to connect with other folks that have the same unyielding love for woodworking as you do here. These contacts can potentially lead to fascinating partnerships on projects or even to establishing the groundwork for brand-new company endeavors. On your path to become a skilled woodworker, the relationships you build with other members of the woodworking community will prove to be a very useful asset.

Gaining Access to Endangered Species of Wood

Certain communities of woodworkers enjoy the privilege of having access to rare or exotic wood species that are not easily accessible on the market. These species are not used very often. Putting your skills as a woodworker to use with these extraordinary materials might pique your creative interest and open up new avenues for you to explore. Because of this privilege, you are able to produce truly one-of-a-kind works, which will distinguish you from other woodworkers.

Support on an emotional level and companionship

When you spend a lot of time in your workshop working on a project, you could get the impression that it's a solitary activity. On the other hand, if you join a community of woodworkers, you will be accepted into a circle of people who share your interests and who are supportive of one another. People who understand the highs and lows, the challenges and accomplishments, and the occasional disappointments that woodworking may offer can be found in this community. Your road toward becoming a better woodworker will be more enjoyable, thanks to the motivation and certainty you gain from having a sense of belonging in the community.

Opportunities to Present Your Work to Others

Last but not least, you'll be able to locate fascinating opportunities to exhibit your projects within groups devoted to woodworking. The members of numerous communities are given the opportunity to display their handiwork through the organization of exhibitions, festivals, and even internet galleries. This exposure not only allows you to display your work, but it also can result in increased recognition and sales or commissions in the future.

It is a wise choice to become a member of a community of woodworkers when you are organizing your woodworking space. It gives access to a world abundant in information, resources, and a helpful community of other people who share the same interests as you. Being a member of a community specializing in woodworking may help speed your learning, feed your creativity, and enrich your entire woodworking experience. This is true regardless of whether you are a beginner just starting in the world of woodworking or an experienced craftsman looking to broaden your horizons. Do not wait; look for a group of woodworkers in your area or join an online community and start developing your wood workshop with a renewed sense of vigor and purpose. Your experience in woodworking will never be the same again after this.

Chapter Four

General tips for shop tool maintenance

The workshop of any skilled carpenter should be scrupulously maintained because it is the craft's beating heart. It is imperative that these tools, which are essential to creative expression, be kept in top condition. In this extensive lesson, we'll go into the vital art of maintaining the shop tools in your woodworking space, which is a skill that's important to have. This kind of maintenance isn't just about preserving instruments; instead, it's about ensuring the longevity of your job, improving the quality of your output, and protecting your health and safety.

The Importance of Tidiness

Imagine that your workshop is an operating room and that cleanliness is the first line of protection against infection. Sawdust, wood chips, and other detritus have no place on a woodworker's equipment; just as a surgeon keeps the operating room clean, a woodworker must do the same. The collection of such debris can severely impair the functionality of a tool. Take some time after each usage to carefully clean your tools, removing any sawdust or wood chips that may have accumulated. Utilize a shop vacuum to reclaim your victory over those difficult-to-reach nooks and crannies hiding these woodworking foes.

The act of greasing

A symphony of moving parts may be found at the core of most of the woodworking tools. Lubrication serves as the conductor of their happy relationship. Be sure to follow the lubricating requirements provided by the maker of your tools to guarantee that they run as smoothly as a well-tuned instrument. When it comes to preventing wear and tear, crucial locations like bearings, slides, and cutting surfaces all require their special elixir, which can be provided by applying lubricants.

Care of the Blade and the Bit

Your cutting tools are the virtuosos of woodworking, and just like any other virtuoso, they need special care and attention to perform at their highest level. Check your saw blades, router bits, and drill bits on a regular basis for telltale signs of wear or dullness. A blade in good condition not only produces cuts that are clean and accurate but also protects its user from potential dangers. Always be on the lookout, and hone or replace your blades and bits as necessary.

The process of aligning and calibrating

The ability to work with precision in woodworking is analogous to that of a maestro's perfect pitch. Cutting and joining with precision requires instruments that have been precisely calibrated. It would help if you regularly checked how aligned your table saw, miter saw, jointer, and planer are. Put yourself in a position to achieve your goals by arming yourself with high-precision measurement tools, such as a precision square or dial indicator. This will allow you to create an environment where your goals and tools coexist perfectly.

Cleaning Up the Dust

The effectiveness of your dust-collecting system has a direct bearing on not just your health but also the health of your tools. An environment that is free of dirt and debris can be maintained in a workshop by ensuring that its dust collecting systems are in good working order. Conduct routine checks on your dust collecting system to ensure it operates at peak efficiency. Don't forget to replace or clean your filters as the manufacturer recommends. When you do so, you safeguard not just your instruments but also your lungs from potential damage.

To Begin With, Safety

When it comes to woodworking, safety measures serve as the introduction to the protective movement. Guards for the blades, safety switches, and other such safeguards must always be in perfect functioning order. It would help if you never tried to go around or get rid of these traits since they are your silent sentinels against danger. If any safety features have been compromised, replace them immediately. Your well-being should always and without fail be your priority.

Keeping It Safe From Rust While Storing It

The enemy of tools, moisture can wreak havoc on their operation and is capable of causing a lot of trouble. Protect your armory by storing your tools somewhere cool and dry to store. You could want to take preventative precautions against rust by using silica gel packs or rust-inhibiting paper, for example. On metal surfaces, a light coat of machine oil applied in a circular motion will create an additional protective barrier against the stealthy progression of rust.

Replace Any Damaged Components

A tool's pieces can deteriorate with time, just like the parts of a live body. Belts, brushes, and electrical components all have a limited amount of time before they need to be replaced. Always watch for telltale signs of wear on your tools, and swiftly replace any worn-out components. This preventative strategy not only prevents more damage but also ensures the highest possible level of performance.

Ongoing Quality Control

The term that best describes your workshop is "vigilance." Instead of waiting until a tool breaks down, start doing inspections regularly. Scrutinize your instruments, looking for even the tiniest traces of wear, damage, or missing components. Finding solutions to problems as soon as they arise will save you time, money and the aggravation of having your work interrupted.

Instructional Methods and Educational Opportunities

Like any other artist, a carpenter's abilities are never truly complete. Spend money on furthering your education. Please get familiar with the fundamental procedures for maintaining your tools, and make it a habit to keep up with the most recent information released by tool manufacturers. To further your awareness of the upkeep of your tools, you can benefit from participating in a workshop or taking a class. Your knowledge is the most powerful instrument in your arsenal.

The meticulous care you take of your tools is the most important factor in running a successful wood workshop. When these general pointers are followed religiously, they will ensure that your tools remain in peak condition, enabling you to produce high-quality woodworking products safely and efficiently. Remember that a well-maintained workshop is a site of creativity and a monument to your unwavering passion for the craft you practice.

Chapter Five

Measuring marking and layout

Here, we will go on a voyage that will take us deep into the spirit of woodworking. In this world, every measurement is a heartbeat, every mark is a stroke of genius, and every plan is a blueprint of dreams.

Selecting the Appropriate Instruments and Reliable Accompanists:

Imagine walking into your very own woodworking shop, the kind of place where aspirations are made real. However, you will need your creative friends and instruments before you can venture into the world of originality. Combination squares, tape measures, calipers, and marking gauges are trustworthy partners that will never betray you in a time of need. These are not merely tools but the instruments you will use to achieve perfection. They differentiate a project from one that is merely functional to one that is an artistic masterpiece in its own right. Invest wisely, as these instruments will be your compass throughout the journey.

Taking Accurate Measures - Where Every Fraction Is Considered Important:

Every centimeter, every inch, and everything in between counts. Accuracy is of the utmost importance when working with wood. Imagine this: you're figuring out how long a delicate tabletop is by measuring its length. Your tape measure has a hook that fits on the edge, and you slide it out from there with the utmost care to ensure it always aligns with the same beginning point. There is complete silence in the room, and the only sound that can be heard is the hissing of your tape measure. You take a number of different measures and cross-check them to guarantee that there is no space for error. Your work stands out from others because of the careful attention to detail that you put into it.

The Marking Process for Accuracy and the Brushstroke of the Artist:

Now, picture taking your accurate measurement and transforming it into a plan that can be implemented. Marking, the artist's brushstroke on the wood or canvas, comes into play. You take your precise marking knife or your sharp pencil, and with steady hands, you carve lines into the wood that will determine its future. These lines are what give the wood its character. Because the angle is ideal, the lines are clear, and they run perpendicular to the surface, you can rest assured that your cuts will be accurate, saving you both time and material.

Plan for Achievement and the Drawing of Your Dreams:

Layout is not only about lines and angles but also about imagining how everything will turn out. Your plan becomes the blueprint to realize your vision for the finished work, which you envision as the finished product. You decide where the joints will meet, where the cuts will be made, and where the design will be most prominent. You begin by lightly sketching your dreams onto the wood with a pencil. You draw bold lines as the vision begins to form, and you do so with the awareness that each contains a piece of your heart.

Utilizing Layout Tools - The Orchestration of a Craftsperson:

Your tools take on the role of an orchestra, with each instrument performing its assigned role to produce a precise symphony. The combination square provides exact angles, the T-square ensures straight lines, and the marking gauge acts as your conductor, directing lines parallel to the edge of your workpiece. All three of these squares are part of a set of three used in woodworking.

Moving the Measurements Around and Establishing Continuity:

But working with wood is much more than just producing distinct pieces; it's also about establishing continuity. For accurate distance measurement and replication, you can utilize dividers like little compasses used in woodworking. You might also use a story stick, which is a physical link between the components, to make sure that each portion is connected to the total in an aesthetically pleasing way.

Take into account the Wood Movement concerning Nature:

In your pursuit of accuracy, you suddenly recall that the wood you are working with is a living organism. It has a pulse, and it moves. Depending on the level of humidity, it will either expand or contract. In light of this, you make adjustments to the markings and layouts so that they take into consideration the characteristics of the material. Your familiarity with wood's natural rhythms assures that your work will withstand the test of time without developing cracks or becoming out of alignment.

The Craftsman's Virtues Lie in Daily Effort and Enduring Tenacity:

It takes practice to become proficient in measuring, marking, and layout, just like with any other creative form. It requires a lot of practice. It requires a lot of patience. You take your time and enjoy the process rather than rushing through it. Not out of an abundance of caution but rather out of reverence for the art form, you take two measurements before making the first cut. You advance with every single measurement, every single mark, and every single layout. You progress from being merely a woodworker to being a craftsperson.

Chapter Six

The Safety Guides

It is imperative to remember that safety is an indispensable travel companion on this adventure. Everyone who works with wood is responsible for ensuring they work in a safe environment, regardless of their experience level. As a result, let's go into an in-depth investigation of the extensive safety rules that will act as your dependable friends as you embark on your woodworking journey.

Personal Protective Equipment, or PPE, includes the following:

Imagine putting on the armor of a modern-day knight; this is what it's like for a woodworker when they put on their protective equipment (PPE). When you put on protective eyewear, such as goggles or safety glasses, you act as a shield against unseen missiles, protecting your eyes from flying debris. Earmuffs and earplugs relieve your auditory system by muffling the din caused by spinning machines. When you put on a dust mask and secure it over your nose and mouth, you not only take in air but also the sense of relief from knowing that minute particles won't be able to enter your lungs.

Putting on Clothes and Shoes:

Imagine that your clothes are a uniform specially tailored for the dance of perfection. It's not just about looking good; it's also about staying safe. Loose clothing becomes dangerous as it engages in the blade-twirling dance, and open-toed shoes might as well be a target for falling equipment. Your choice of appropriate apparel, including garments that fit you snugly and shoes with closed toes and gripping soles, should become your ally to ensure that every step and movement you make is steady and safe.

Organization of the Workspace:

Think of your workstation as a blank canvas, ready for you to turn your thoughts into something tangible. However, to succeed in woodworking, you must maintain a tidy environment, much like an artist needs a clean palette. Keeping workbenches, supplies, and equipment in order is not only suitable for the aesthetics of the space; it also helps prevent accidents. Getting rid of the clutter eliminates the risk of tripping over anything and frees up your attention and energy to focus entirely on the activity.

Concerning Equipment:

Imagine that your instruments are an extension of your hands, only they are more powerful and precise. To properly and securely wield them is a skill unto itself. Maintaining their cleanliness and sharpness may seem tedious, but it demonstrates your artistry and is a preventative measure against unneeded accidents. Properly storing these items when they are not in use is a matter of cleanliness and of making a safe covenant, ensuring that no oblivious hands or feet will come into unintended contact with their edges.

Security of the Machine

The force and precision of the machinery in a carpentry shop are comparable to that of a symphony. However, in the same way that a conductor follows a score, you must follow the instructions provided by the maker very carefully. Reading is only the beginning; you also need to comprehend the complexities of the setup, the intricate dance of modifications, and the critical role that safety features play. Because of this harmony, the roar of each machine contributes to the overall symphony of safety.

Ventilation, as well as a Dust Collection System

Imagine your workshop as an ecosystem where the air quality is an essential component that cannot be compromised. Even though it's a satisfying hobby, working with wood generates a lot of dust and can sometimes even be toxic. Having adequate ventilation is a trustworthy bodyguard, ensuring the air you breathe is uncontaminated and unrestricted. A dust collection system functions similarly to a diligent butler in that it gathers every speck of dust, ensuring that the air and your lungs remain unburdened.

Prevention of Fires:

The woodshop is a haven for creative thought, but creative thought may also cause sparks to fly — sometimes quite literally. An extinguisher is a watchful guard, protecting against fires that may break out unexpectedly. Imagine it as your collaborator in putting down any raging revolt and preserving the peace and safety of the environment.

Security in Electrical Systems:

A workshop is alive with the hum of electricity, which moves across the space like an invisible yet potent conductor. It is up to you to ensure that the performance is harmonic and not chaotic. Be a watchful guardian and check the cords for frays and damage. Additionally, give the grounded outlets a nod of approval. Avoid doing this at all costs since overloading circuits has the same effect as placing an excessive load on the conductor. Remember that moisture and electricity do not get along well, so ensure your workspace is always dry to avoid unanticipated sparks.

Protection against Chemicals:

Consider chemicals to be the equivalent of the alchemical components that are needed for your woodworking spells. It would help to treat them with care, much like a potion master would, because they can be dangerous. The original containers continue to serve as their charmed vessels, protecting them from the glare of the sun and the intense heat. When dealing with these concoctions, make sure your workspace is a place that has adequate ventilation.

First Aid and Preparation for Emergencies:

A well-stocked first aid kit is a secret treasure that every woodworker ought to have in their possession. Imagine it as a magical elixir you always have ready to use in case of any tiny disasters. Create a contingency plan, and do it like an explorer would map unexplored territory. This map outlines potential escape routes and lists reliable contacts that could save your life in an emergency.

Education and On-the-Job-Training:

Safety will be your constant companion on your journey through the world of woodworking. Participate in seminars, immerse yourself in courses, and attend workshops if you want to maintain your competitive edge. Learning is a torch that illuminates the route to safety, keeping you current with the latest practices and ensuring that you are not just a woodworker but a diligent guardian of your craft. Learning keeps you informed with the newest practices and ensures you are a guardian of your art.

Safety is not a choice but an absolute need when dealing with wood. The things you use, like tools and materials, are an extension of your creativity and the precautions you take to become an oath to honor and safeguard that creation. As you give your woodworking projects the breath of life, make safety the constant heartbeat that assures each venture is a masterpiece of innovation and security.

Book 2:
Tools

Introduction

Whether you're a seasoned pro or just getting started, a well-equipped woodworking shop is essential for putting your passion into tangible results. The tools that are more than simply tools and are extensions of your abilities and creativity are the focus as we delve into the heart of your woodworking environment. Sawdust and machine noise aside, your workshop is where innovations in thought and execution take form. Get inspired and get things done in the woodworking space of your dreams with the guidance of this book. Woodworking as an art form has been practiced for centuries, yet its methods have evolved with time. Traditional workmanship has been updated with modern technologies without losing its soul. We open the door to a world where everything you use is designed to accomplish a certain job. We cover everything from the intricacies of workstation selection to the intricate ballet of hand tools and power equipment. Everything from selecting the right tool for the job to maintaining it afterward is covered in this comprehensive guide. The foundation of your workshop is where your ambitious projects—like elaborate furniture, intricate figurines, or practical household items—are born. Wood, tools, and a shared vision: Here we go!

Chapter One:

Hand Tools

You have entered the fantastic realm of woodworking, where the success of your practical masterpieces depends on the skill you develop in your private workshop. This first section of our "Woodworking Bible" leads you by the hand and shows you how to use the fundamental equipment to make your woodworking goals a reality. Envision yourself venturing into the fascinating world of hand tools, where every implement becomes a vehicle for your imagination and a link to the pioneers of this time-honored profession.

The Essential Hand Tools for Any Serious Woodworker:

Chisels - Your Artist's Palette:

If you think of a chisel used in woodworking as a paintbrush, you'll start to see the point. Like an artist's palette, this collection of vast and varied tools allows you to carve, shape, and enhance your wooden paintings with pinpoint accuracy. Mortise chisels are the sculptor's tools, carving joints with a steady hand, while paring chisels, which resemble fine-tipped brushes, allow you to execute intricate work.

Handsaws: The Melody of Cutting:

A woodworker's handsaw is like a violinist's bow; without it, they couldn't create the most beautiful music out of wood. A crosscut saw rip saw, and dovetail saw all play complementary roles in the cutting process. Saws with teeth so sharp that they sing when they cut wood are worth the investment if you want your cuts to look and feel like the work of a master artisan.

Planes - The Artisan's Best Friend:

When it comes to smoothing and flattening wood, your trusty friends in woodworking are the hand planes. You can pick up a jointer plane, a block plane, or a smoothing plane. Use them to give your works of art a spark of life and polish them until they shine like crystals.

Tools for Marking and Measuring - The Architects of Precision:

Accuracy is of the utmost importance in woodworking. Think of your marking and measuring tools as the architects who ensure every piece of wood fits perfectly. You may rely on your combination square, marking gauge, and sliding bevel gauge for this precise work.

Screwdrivers - The Unseen Architects:

Despite the prevalence of power tools, woodworking still values the knowledge gained through practice and experience. Screwdrivers are the unsung heroes of the woodworking world, turning screws with the finesse of a symphony conductor. Your projects will be in harmony with the help of your notes, which come in various sizes and forms.

Mallets and Hammers - The Conductors of Impact:

To visualize the impact of your woodworking, think of mallets and hammers as conductors. They wield chisels like a conductor's baton, driving them with pinpoint accuracy to ensure perfect joint alignment. Mallets made of wood or rubber are soft yet sturdy, protecting your tools and the wood from damage, and claw hammers are always ready to take on the conductor job.

Files and Rasps - Sculptors of Detail:

Sculptors in the world of wood, these instruments smooth and shape surfaces where planes and sandpaper would fear to tread. Files and rasps add an aesthetic touch, bringing out the delicate beauty of your creations' hidden curves and complicated regions.

Tools for Carving - Paintbrushes:

Those interested in woodcarving will find that a set of carving tools opens up a world of beautiful and complex designs. These implements, which come in a wide range of sizes and forms and are reminiscent of an artist's brushes, will take your woodworking to a new level.

Clamps, the Stability Watchdogs:

Clamps may not be tools in the traditional sense, but they are essential to keeping your workshop steady. They provide a haven for your creations, keeping them steady as you bring your ideas to life. Bar, C-clamps, and pipe clamps play different parts in your woodworking symphony.

Sharpening Tools - The Keepers of Precision:

Finally, sharpening tools are the guardians of accuracy in your workshop. You may keep your hand tools as sharp as a master's wit with sharpening stones, honing guides, and a strop. After all, sharpness is the essence of class in woodworking.

Chapter Two

Power Tools

Power tools are the tireless steeds that take your ambitions and aspirations into the realm of concrete beauty in woodworking. They are the tools that make your visions a reality. These incredible pieces of technology have the potential to become your reliable allies and give life to your projects. However, individuals just starting this adventure may initially appear to be terrifying animals. Let's adventure into the world of power tools used in woodworking. We aim to see these tools not as simple equipment but as extensions of your art and imagination.

1. The Circular Saw, a Performer of Unmatched Accuracy:

A circular saw is analogous to a painter's brush with a sharp point because it enables you to cut through the wood canvas with the precision of an operating knife. Its circular blade, which can spin at breakneck speed, is your ace in the hole when making straight and precise cuts across various wood kinds. If you ever find yourself in a situation where you need to cut large sheets of plywood into more manageable pieces or if you want to make long rip cuts, the circular saw will be your most reliable ally. Look for one that enables you to change the cutting depth and the angle of the edge; this will give you much more flexibility in designing your projects.

2. The Table Saw: The Master of Accuracy:

The table saw is the conductor of accuracy in the woodworking orchestra and takes center stage in the woodworking process. Its table is perfectly level and unyielding, making it the ideal setting for a circular saw blade that can be lifted, lowered, and slanted to perform rip cuts (along the length of the wood) and crosscuts (across the breadth of the wood) with unmatched accuracy. If you take good care of your table saw, it will become an enduring friend who will be there for you for many years.

3. Compound Miter Saw, often known as the Angle Artisan:

A compound miter saw is like an artist's brush since it allows them to design cuts at such precise angles. Bevel cuts are made at an angle through the thickness of the wood, while miter cuts are made at an angle across the width of the wood. This blade moves beautifully through moldings, trims, and frame components, making the transition between the two types of cuts seem effortless. Your level of craftsmanship will be elevated thanks to newer models integrated with laser guides. These guides make every cut more accurate.

4. Router, also known as the Wizard's Wand:

In the toolbox of a woodworker, the router is the equivalent of a magic wand. They carve grooves into the wood, make beautiful edges, and mold the material into gorgeous shapes using quickly spinning bits. Routers can turn plain boards into pieces of beauty by bestowing beautiful patterns upon them. This can be accomplished by routing intricate patterns into the boards. They provide varied degrees of control and become your artistic partner, regardless of whether you hold them in your hand or place them on a table.

5. Jigsaw, also known as "The Sculptor's Hand":

The sculptor's hand is transformed into a jigsaw, which brings delicate curves and complicated designs to reality. Because of its thin, reciprocating blade, it is possible to make precise hand-guided cuts, making it the ideal instrument for cutting delicate patterns and templates for custom furniture or plywood. The jigsaw transforms into your chisel and turns your concept into a tangible form, regardless of whether you are an amateur or an expert.

6. The Drill Press, also known as The Precision Architect:

When it comes to woodworking, precision is of the utmost importance, especially when drilling holes for joinery and installing tools. The drill press provides both the precision and the efficiency required for these operations due to its robust base and adjustable drill head. It turns into an architectural tool for you, allowing you to make sure each hole is drilled exactly where you want it to be. There are also speed settings, and depth stops on some models of drill presses, which further enhance your control.

7. The Electric Drill, a Versatile and Masterful Tool:

A cordless power drill is the ultimate multi-tool, a virtuoso capable of doing more than just drilling holes in things. It becomes your companion in driving screws and nuts, providing control by allowing you to modify the speed and the force of the driving action. When you have this instrument in your hand, you can secure, tighten, and fasten, and you can do it with the confidence that each of these actions is at your command.

8. The Random Orbital Sander, Also Known as the Craftsman's Final Touch:

Creating a masterpiece requires more than just cutting and sculpting; it also requires the careful attention that comes with finishing. Your canvas will retain its professional appearance even after the random orbital sander has finished its elliptical dance across the material's surface. It takes on the form of the brush used by a trained craftsman, guaranteeing that the surface of your work is as even and smooth as if a professional had painted it.

9. Belt Sanders, also known as the Material Mover:

When there is a pressing need to quickly remove a significant quantity of material, the belt sander steps into the spotlight. Flattening surfaces, smoothing edges, and even generating bends in more significant parts are all possible thanks to the machine's rapidly moving abrasive belt. However, similar to a mighty steed, it demands respect and attention because of its potentially hostile nature if it is not managed carefully.

10. The Wood Whisperers' Planer and Jointer:

Planers and jointers are the "whisperers of transformation" working with rough-sawn wood since they smooth the material's surface. While the jointer ensures that one side and one edge of a board are flat and square, the planer ensures that the thickness is consistent throughout. These tools are the architects of precise joinery, ensuring your results are smooth and professional, a testament to your craftsmanship.

When working with wood, power tools are more than just instruments; they are extensions of your artistry and imagination. They increase your potential, but with that power comes the obligation to put your safety first. Put on the necessary protective gear, pay attention to the instructions provided by the manufacturer, and work slowly to get the hang of these tools. Not only will you be able to create beautiful things out of wood, but you will also be able to leave behind a legacy of craft if you have the necessary skills, respect, and tools.

Chapter Three

Stationary and Machine Tools

Stationary Tools

Workbench: The workbench is the heart of your workplace. It gives you a stable and large place to work on various projects. It's more than just a table; it's your most essential tool. Consider size, stability, and work holding options when picking the proper workbench for your room and projects. Traditional woodworking benches often have vises and dog holes for clamping. Modern versions may have built-in storage options.

Miter Saw Station: You need a miter saw to make correct crosscuts and cuts at an angle. Invest in a specialized miter saw station with extensions to hold longer work to maximize its use. This setting makes your workshop more precise and safer.

Router Table: A router table is essential for shaping edges, making complicated profiles, and doing accurate joinery work. Look for one that can be changed and use different router bits. With this tool, you can get professional-quality finishing.

Drill Press: A drill press is used when it's important to make holes with the same depth and angle every time. It's a must-have for typical woodworking jobs like putting in dowels and boring holes for hardware. Make sure your drill press has features like speed controls and accurate depth stops.

Machines Tools

Table Saw: A table saw is the heart of most woodworking shops. It is excellent for ripping wood, making crosscuts, and making complex joints. Safety features, like blade guards and riving knives, are very important to stay safe and make precise cuts. Choose a table saw that fits your needs for work and accuracy.

Jointer: A jointer flattens and lines the edges of rough lumber to be worked on further. This is a must-do step before joining flat areas together. Look for models with movable tables and a spiral cutter head for better results.

Planer: A planer works with a joiner to ensure all your wood is the same thickness. This is very important for making boards that are the right size and have no flaws. Look for planers that are easy to change and built well.

Band Saw: A band saw is a flexible tool that can cut curves complex shapes, and even resaw thicker pieces of wood into thinner ones. It gives your crafting projects a whole new look. When picking a band saw, you should consider its throat capacity, motor power, and general stability.

Lathe: A lathe is an essential tool for anyone who wants to turn wood. It lets you make symmetrical patterns and make bowls, spindle legs, and decorative pieces out of wood. Choose a lathe whose motor speed and bed length are suitable for the size of your projects.

Getting the right tools for your wood shop is the first step on your journey as a woodworker. Stationary and machine tools are the backbone of your creative space. They help you do everything from making accurate joints to shaping complex designs. As you start this woodworking project, remember that the quality of your tools significantly affects how well your work turns out. Invest carefully, put safety first, and let the quality of your work show.

Book 3: Techniques

Introduction

Your well-equipped workshop is your safe place where raw materials can be turned into beautiful things through the alchemy of skill and vision. This book is more than just a guide; it's the key to your woodworking journey's full potential. From the basics to the finer points, this book will guide you through the complex process of setting up and improving your wood workshop. As we go through the following parts, you'll find a treasure trove of tips for new and experienced woodworkers. We'll talk about how to choose the right tools, set them up in your place, and master the techniques that bring wood to life. All these things will find a place in your woodworking arsenal: the subtleties of grain, the beauty of joinery, and the symphony of finishes. But this book is more than just a technology guide. It's a friend who understands every woodworker's passion and commitment. We know the joy of making the first bit of sawdust, the thrill of a joint that fits perfectly, and the satisfaction of finishing a job that shows off your skills.

This book will help you every step of the way, whether you want to make intricate furniture pieces, useful everyday things, or artistic expressions of your energy. From planning your workshop layout to the final touches, we're here to ensure your way is well-lit and the results are better than you expected. So, dear reader, get ready to go on a journey of craftsmanship, skill, and self-discovery, whether setting up your first wood workshop or improving one you already have. The pages after this one are for you, your love, and the art that comes to life in wood. Where your crafting dreams start, your shop becomes where masterpiece after masterpiece is made.

Chapter One

Preparing Woods

Woodworking is an art that blends skill, precision, and creativity. But before you make beautiful things out of wood, you need to know the most basic part of woodworking: preparing your wood. We'll review the most important ways to pick, handle, and prepare wood for your woodworking projects.

Selecting the Right Wood:

The first step for every carpenter is to choose the suitable wood for the job. This choice can make or break your project, so it's essential to understand different types of woodwork.

Hardwood vs. Softwood: Start by telling the difference between hardwoods and softwoods. Hardwoods like oak, maple, and cherry are durable and great for making furniture, while softwoods like pine and cedar are great for outdoor projects. Hardwoods are usually denser and more muscular, which makes them suitable for load-bearing buildings. Softwoods, on the other hand, are lighter and usually easier to work with.

Grading and Quality: Once you've chosen between hardwood and softwood, it's essential to know how to identify wood grades, as they show the quality and appearance of the wood. Grading standards can differ based on where you live, but they usually include categories like Select, No. 1 Common, and No. 2 Common. Higher-grade wood usually has fewer flaws and a more uniform look, which can be necessary for exemplary woodworker projects.

Moisture Content: Wood is a hygroscopic material that can absorb or release moisture based on its surroundings. The amount of water in wood is a key factor in how it behaves during and after woodworking. Too wet or dry wood can cause problems like warping, cracks, or joints that don't hold. Get a wetness meter to make sure your wood is ready to use. This tool will help you determine if the wood is at the right moisture level for your job. Wood for indoor projects should generally have a moisture content of around 6-8%, while wood for outdoor projects should be around 12-15%.

Wood Preparation Techniques:

Once you've chosen the suitable wood, it's time to prepare it for your woodworking job. Here are some essential tips:

Planing and Milling: To prepare your wood for milling, you need to plan it to the right thickness and smoothness. A planer and a jointer are essential tools for this process. Planers are used to lower the thickness of your wood, making it uniform and smooth.

On the other hand, jointers are used to flatten one side of the wood and make a straight edge to guide further shape. Planning and milling ensure your wood is flat, straight, and ready for further shape.

Cutting and Sawing: Accurate cutting is a crucial part of woodworking. Use different saws like circular, jigsaws, and hand saws to make exact cuts based on your project plans. You must measure and mark your wood correctly to make joints that fit well and look good.

Joinery: This is the art of combining pieces of wood to make solid and long-lasting joints. Some standard joinery methods are dovetails, mortise and tenon, and doweling. The choice of joinery relies on the needs of your project. It is essential to know how to use these methods and when to use them if you want to make woodwork that is both strong and looks good.

Sanding and finishing: The final step in preparing wood is to get a smooth, shiny surface. Sanding smoothing the wood by removing flaws and preparing the surface for finishing. Start with coarse-grit sandpaper and gradually move to smaller grits for a smooth finish. After cleaning, you can finish your wood with stains, varnishes, or paints to protect and improve its look. The choice of finish depends on the type of wood and how you want the job to look when it's done.

Handling and Security:

For woodworking, you need solid tools and sharp blades. Safety should always be the top priority:

Safety Gear: Invest in safety gear like safety glasses, hearing protection, and dust masks. These things protect you from flying wood chips, loud machines, and harmful dust particles.

Maintenance: Make sure you maintain your tools regularly to keep them in the best shape possible. Broken or worn-out tools can cause crashes and lower the quality of your work. Keep your cutting edges sharp and replace or fix any broken parts.

Workshop Organization: Keep your workshop well-organized to reduce the chance of accidents. Properly storing and labeling your tools and materials can save time and keep your area safe. Also, ensure your work area is well-lit, and all cords and hoses are properly secured to avoid tripping risks.

Learning to choose, handle, and prepare wood will lay a strong foundation for your woodworking journey.

Chapter Two

Joinery Techniques

In essence, joinery is the sculptor's touch on wood, the art of making strong and aesthetically attractive linkages. While nails and screws are helpful, they do not have the elegance and grace that excellent joinery provides to a project. Joinery pours new life into wood, creating linkages that appear to be pre-ordained by nature.

Mortise and Tenon Joints: Think of this traditional joint as a tight hug between two old friends. Like an outstretched hand, the tenon slides effortlessly into the welcoming mortise, providing a solid but harmonious connection. This technique is frequently used to create strong table legs or the lovely curves of a chair's frame. It exemplifies strength and stability.

Dovetail joints are similar to the delicate interlocking fingers of a skilled pianist. These joints are more than just functional; they are works of art. They are frequently found adorning drawers and boxes, leaving an unmistakable signature of craftsmanship that transcends usefulness and borders on poetry.

 Butt Joints: The rustic handshake of woodworking, butt joints are simple in its simplest form. Two pieces of wood come together at a square angle, often reinforced with screws, nails, or glue. While not visually appealing, they perform their duty with understated grace.

Rabbet Joints: Rabbet joints resemble a love embrace in joinery, where one piece of wood gently overlaps another, forming a secure groove. These joints, frequently used in constructing cabinet backs or providing rigidity to drawer bottoms, are a testament to functionality meeting artistry.

Tongue and Groove Joints: Tongue and groove joints are like secret conversations between old friends. They fit together perfectly, creating a smooth surface that screams precision and excellence. These joints ensure an even level of harmony in wood floors, paneling, or tabletops.

The Tool Symphony:

The beauty of joinery extends to the tools themselves, each a distinct instrument in the orchestra of a carpenter.

Chisels: These unsung warriors carefully carve mortises and detail, shaping wood like a sculptor's hand.

Mallets: Like a conductor maintaining the subtleties of a musical piece, mallets provide the soft conductor's touch, directing chisels and tools with a grace that prevents injury to the wood.

Precision saws, like a virtuoso's bow, provide the clean, melodic cuts required to create harmonious, snug connections.

Marking and Measuring Tools: Squares, rulers, and marking gauges serve as navigational aids for the carpenter, ensuring that every cut is a note in a symphony of perfection.

Patience and Practice are at the heart of joinery.

Joinery transcends basic techniques in the holy grounds of the wood workshop; it is an art form that requires patience and unending effort. Woodworkers spend years honing their craft, learning to listen to the whispers of the wood and feel its grain in the same way musicians feel the beat in their bones. Each joint tells a tale in the silent language of wood, where every cut bears the weight of history and perfection reigns supreme.

Joinery's Legacies:

Joinery's continuing appeal stems from its ability to bridge the gap between the past and the present. Traditional woodworking techniques are passed down through generations, like the pages of a treasured family album. They maintain the wisdom and creativity of previous woodworkers, reminding us of the traditions that underpin the profession. Handcrafted joinery remains a mark of excellence, a reference to the craft's enduring tradition, even in today's world of advanced machines and mass manufacturing.

Chapter Three

Sanding and Finishing Techniques

Every woodworker has an unquenchable passion for crafting unfinished lumber into beautiful works of art. Whether a strong piece of furniture, an exquisite carving, or a stunning cabinet, creating a wooden masterpiece takes skill and knowledge of the delicate yet transformative procedures of sanding and finishing. These methods, which are frequently disregarded, have the potential to turn your woodworking projects from ordinary to spectacular. Join us on this tour through the wood shop as we explore the tools, processes, and tricks used in sanding and finishing to transform unfinished wood into priceless art pieces.

The Basis: Appropriate Preparation

Establishing a solid foundation is essential before we begin the art of sanding and polishing. Wood must be adequately prepared to receive the finishing touches, just as an artist primes their canvas. You must choose the ideal wood for your project, ensure it's dry and seasoned, and thoroughly check it for flaws or faults.

Choosing the Right Wood: Selecting the wood is the first step in any woodworking job. The sort of wood you select will significantly impact the result. Each wood species has a distinct hardness, color, and grain pattern. Knowing your wood well is the first step to producing a masterpiece; it's similar to understanding the qualities of a superb wine.

Drying and seasoning: Since wood is a living substance, its moisture content is essential. To prevent warping or splitting when the process is finished, be sure the wood has been thoroughly dried and seasoned. To make sure the wood is prepared, use a moisture meter.

Check your wood for knots, cracks, and other flaws affecting the final product. While certain flaws give something character, others might need to be fixed or avoided in your design.

The Art of Refinement: Sanding

Sanding is like polishing a rough diamond for a carpenter. It's a process that calls for perseverance, accuracy, and the appropriate equipment. Sanding makes the wood smoother and prepares it to absorb the finish.

Choosing Sandpaper: Sandpaper is available in various coarse and fine grits. Coarser grits (lower numbers) are employed for heavy stock removal, but finer grits (higher numbers) produce a smoother surface. As you work toward the ideal smoothness, start with coarse grit and move to finer grits.

Sanding techniques: To avoid unsightly scratches, always sand with the grain of the wood. To create a uniform finish, use even pressure and keep a constant motion.

Sanding in stages: To have a smooth, silky surface, start with a coarser grit (like 80) and progressively work up to finer grits (like 120 and 220). The key to a faultless finish is this methodical tweaking.

Adding the Final Touch: Giving Wood Life

Your wood is prepared for its final treatment after the thorough sanding procedure. Wood finishing protects the wood, enhances its attractiveness, and adds depth and character, among other vital functions.

Different wood finishes exist, including lacquer, water-based, and oil-based. Everyone has advantages and uses. While water-based finishes are quick-drying and ecologically friendly, oil-based finishes provide a warm, classic appearance. Lacquer offers a glossy, long-lasting finish.

Application Methods: Depending on the finish type you select, there are different application techniques. Tools, including brushes, rags, and spray cans, are typical. Always adhere to the application and drying instructions provided by the manufacturer.

Patience and Multiple Coats: Often, it takes several coats to get a perfect finish. Between layers, softly sand the surface using fine-grit sandpaper to prepare it for the next application. Patience throughout this phase is essential because hurrying can result in errors.

Sanding and finishing are acts of workmanship in the woodworking shop rather than merely procedures in a project. They are the last touches of the artist's brush, giving a piece of wood life and personality. Accept the subtleties, make quality tool purchases, and give yourself the time and persistence to become proficient in these techniques. Doing this will release woodworking's full potential and turn unfinished wood into heirloom pieces that future generations will treasure.

Chapter Four

Essential woodworking techniques

Making beautiful, usable items with two hands is profoundly fulfilling in an age of mass production and disposable things. Woodworking has been passed down centuries, evolving into a rich tapestry of methods and skills. Whether you're a novice or an experienced craftsperson, imagination meets workmanship in the wood workshop. In this post, we'll delve into the fundamental woodworking skills that serve as the cornerstone of this art, providing you with a guiding light on your path to becoming a skilled carpenter.

1. Wood Preparation and Selection

Every woodworking job begins with the selection of the appropriate wood. From the rich grains of oak to the smooth smoothness of maple, each wood species has its particular features. When selecting a material, remember the intended purpose, durability, and aesthetics. Take note of the grain patterns, knots, and moisture level, as these characteristics significantly impact the wood's workability.

Proper wood preparation is essential before you begin cutting and shaping. This includes measuring, labeling, and squaring the wood to ensure it is defect-free. Investing time now can save you hours of frustration later on.

2. Marking and Measuring

A skilled woodworker is known for their precision. A good project requires precise measuring and marking. Invest in good measurement instruments, such as a combination square and a trustworthy tape measure. Mark with a sharp point pencil, and always measure twice before cutting. Take your time because errors committed here can be difficult or impossible to correct later.

3. Cutting Methods

Once the wood is ready, you must learn how to cut. Cross-cutting, ripping, and mitering are three primary cutting techniques.

- Cutting across the grain is what cross-cutting entails. Use a sharp cross-cut or table saw with a cross-cut sled for clean, precise cuts.
- The process of cutting along the grain is known as ripping. A rip saw or table saw equipped with a rip fence will assist you in making straight, parallel cuts.
- Mitering is cutting wood at an angle, usually 45 degrees. Perfect angles and tight joins need a miter saw, or a miter box and hand saw.

4. carpenter

Joinery is the art of joining together pieces of wood. Proper joinery ensures that your projects are both functional and long-lasting. Among the most common joinery techniques are:

- Dovetail joints: Dovetail joints are known for their strength and beauty and are used for drawer building and other applications that require a firm binding.
- Mortise and tenon joints are versatile and can be utilized for various projects ranging from tables to chairs.
- Biscuit joinery is excellent for matching edges and making solid connections between boards.

5. Sanding and finishing

A woodworking project's finishing touches can make or ruin it. Sanding is essential for creating a smooth, level surface. Begin with coarse-grit sandpaper and work your way up to finer grits. Apply a high-quality finish such as varnish, shellac, or wax to maintain the wood and enhance its natural beauty.

6. Safety and Tool Maintenance

If safety precautions are not taken seriously, woodworking can be dangerous. Wear safety eyewear, hearing protection, and a dust mask. To ensure precision and safety, keep your tools sharp and well-maintained.

Book 4:
Woods

Introduction

In the mesmerizing world of woodworking, a bond between craftspeople and their materials transcends the ordinary. Imagine, if you will, the scent of freshly cut wood, the texture of the grain beneath your fingertips, and the symphony of saws and chisels coming together in harmony. At the heart of this enchanting realm lies a pivotal choice that weaves a thread through every creation: the choice of wood.

Chapter One

Woods

A woodworker's workshop is a haven full of possibilities, a meeting ground for art and skill. The wood workshop is a monument to human ingenuity and the everlasting appeal of nature's wealth, a place where the timeless beauty of wood is brought to life by expert hands. Here in this holy place, we delve into the beautiful world of woods, learning about their natural characteristics, the skill of careful selection, and the enchantment of transformation. Every wood plank is special in its own way, whether made of oak, maple, cherry, or walnut. The first order of business for a woodworker is to tune in to the grain and color patterns hiding just below the bark. Wood's intricate patterns become stories, knots become idiosyncrasies, and colors become emotions when you learn to read them in the workshop. This is when the woodworker truly works in tandem with nature.

Selecting the suitable wood requires a delicate tango of instinct and expertise. Choosing a piece that fits in with the overall vibe of what you're making is just as important as picking the appropriate type. The skilled artisan recognizes that the beauty of the finished product is dependent on the quality of the wood used and that this involves thinking about more than simply the wood's visual appeal.

Saws, planes, and chisels are brought out once the wood has been selected and the workshop comes to life. It's a harmonious display of skill. Every cut, every carve, and every sanding stroke is a step toward unveiling the wood's hidden beauty as it is transformed from a rough plank to a masterfully carved item. Woodworkers find peace and fulfillment in the meditative pace of their work in the workshop.

A woodworker's goals are to create something beautiful out of the wood and to keep the wood's inherent qualities intact. The finish, be it a glossy varnish or an all-natural oil, is selected to highlight the natural beauty of the wood without masking its unique personality. It's tricky to strike the right chord between encouraging growth and encouraging individuality. Aspirations take form in the workshop. You can turn any ordinary chair into a throne, any ordinary table into a social hub, and any ordinary cabinet into a priceless heirloom. A carpenter creates more than just furniture; they create tales, moments, and memories with each piece. The dedication and care put into each item speaks volumes about the art form's popularity.

The woodshop is an adventure into the wild, not merely a place to make things. In this utopia, time stands still, and every second counts toward the goal of perfection. Sawdust wafts through the air, and the voices of skilled workers past may still be heard. It's a place where trees come to life and share their stories with everyone who cares to listen. The woodshop is an oasis of handcrafting in an age of industrialization and mass production. It's a reminder that machines cannot make everything; sometimes, the human touch makes all the difference. So the next time you enter a woodshop, take a moment to admire the magic that happens there, where the eternal beauty of woods is lovingly brought to life by talented hands and dreams are fashioned into reality.

Chapter Two

Softwoods

The choice of material can make all the difference in the lovely realm of woodworking, where talent and inspiration combine. Because of their strength and beauty, hardwoods have been in the spotlight for a long time. However, softwoods are the workshop's unsung heroes. These gentle giants bring their distinct charm to the creating table, opening up a world of possibilities for seasoned and novice artisans.

Softwoods are derived from trees that are not conifers, as the name implies. They are well-known for their friendliness and warmth. When you run your fingers over softwood, it's as if you're feeling nature itself. It isn't easy to get the same feeling from anything else. One of the best aspects of softwoods is their versatility. They come in various varieties, each with its personality. Pine, spruce, cedar, and fir are some of the most well-known options. These woods are not only easy to work with but can also be shaped into anything your imagination can conjure up.

Softwoods are like a blank canvas waiting to be painted on by a master. They are easy to form and ideal for delicate carvings and joinery work. Softwoods are your workshop best friends, whether you're building a delicate cabinet, a rustic dinner table, or a cute wooden toy. Hardwoods are noted for their strength and density. However, softwoods differ in that they are lighter. As a result, they are ideal for tasks that require portability without sacrificing aesthetics. Consider a handcrafted picnic table that you can move around your yard or a set of adorable wooden seats that you can relocate to your favorite reading location.

The aroma of softwoods transports you to a pine forest or a calm room lined with cedar. This aroma isn't simply pleasant to smell; it may also be used well. Because cedar naturally repels insects, it is frequently used to construct closets and chests. Softwoods are an excellent choice in today's society when sustainability is critical. Because they grow faster than oaks, there are many to pick from. Furthermore, ethical forestry practices ensure that softwood harvesting is environmentally friendly and that these forests are preserved for future generations.

When working with softwoods, various issues arise. They are softer than hard timbers and are more readily dented and scratched. However, this makes them easier to cut, shape, and sand to perfection. To be effective, you must understand how each type of wood works and select the appropriate species for your project. A skillful craftsman understands how to highlight the benefits of softwoods while concealing their shortcomings.

Chapter Three

Hardwoods

Hardwoods are a material in the woodworking field that has endured the test of time because of their strength, beauty, and skilled craftsmanship. Artisans have been captivated by these exceptional woods' distinctive personality and adaptability for millennia. Let us enter the sacred space of the woodshop and go into the world of hardwoods, where each cut, each joint, and each piece holds the weight of history and the promise of timeless beauty.

Hardwood comes from deciduous trees, the towering conifers that lose their leaves each autumn as the seasons change. Hardwoods, in contrast to their softwood cousins, develop slowly, giving them a solid, strong composition. We use finer woods for our workbenches: oak, maple, cherry, walnut, and mahogany.

When discussing hardwoods, glossing over their remarkable strength and longevity is impossible. They're a gift from Mother Nature to the artisan community because of how well they hold up over time. Hardwoods are distinguished from one another by their individual qualities. For example, oak is highly regarded for its durability and attractive grain pattern. However, elaborate designs require the fine, homogeneous texture that maple provides. With its rich, crimson tones, Cherry matures gracefully and becomes more beautiful with time.

Working with hardwoods is a delicate ballet that calls for a master's skill, patience, and familiarity with the wood's unique characteristics. Each joint is a labor of love, and each cut is an act of dedication. Working with hardwoods demands delicacy and refinement that can only be gained through practice. There are advantages and disadvantages to every type of hardwood. Walnut's dark, luxurious tones are appealing, but the wood is notoriously difficult to work with. To bring out its full beauty, the distinctive grain pattern of mahogany wood must be carefully oriented. Learning everything there is to know about working with hardwoods is a never-ending process.

Woodworkers can look to the future of sustainable craft in the hardwoods they use in their workshops today. To guarantee that future generations of craftspeople have access to these natural riches, they must be harvested and sourced sustainably. Many modern woodworkers use reclaimed hardwoods or those recognized by responsible forestry organizations because of their high sustainability standards. We are constantly reminded of the boundless potential of these hardwood marvels as we stand amidst them in our wood workshop. Anything from elaborate inlays to sturdy, heirloom-quality furniture is possible; the only limitation is the craftsman's ingenuity.

Finally, in a woodshop, hardwoods are more than just materials; they constitute the very essence of the craft itself. They link us to the past craftspeople who, like us, strived to create lasting works of art from raw materials. They push us to perfect our techniques, hone our focus, and make things with lasting cultural significance. May the timeless elegance and unrivaled strength that hardwoods contribute to our trade continue to inspire and guide our hands as we carve out a place for woodworking in the world's future.

Chapter Four

Veneers

In the world of woodworking, where every piece is a testament to skill and expertise, veneers have a special place. Thin pieces of wood have been used to make wooden things look better and more useful for many years. Some people might think of veneers as a short-cut, but real artisans and artists know that working with veneers in a wood shop is an exact and laborious process. We'll learn a lot about veneers in this post. We'll look at their past, the art of making them, and the beauty they add to woodworking.

How Veneers Came to Be

The art of veneering goes back to ancient Egypt, where it was used to add beautiful wooden decorations to the tombs of pharaohs. From Greece to Rome, this method spread through different cultures and countries. It reached its peak during the Renaissance. During this time in Europe, the art of marquetry, which uses thin veneers to decorate, grew. It was used to decorate the insides of palaces and churches.

Veneers have been used for a long time because they highlight wood's natural beauty by highlighting its grain patterns, colors, and textures. In a time when ecology is vital, veneers are an intelligent way to get the most out of limited wood resources. A small piece of high-quality wood can cover a more extensive area as a veneer. This makes sure that the best woods are used to their full potential.

Craftsmanship in Veneering

When working with veneers, you must be gentle and pay close attention to the details. Let's look at the hard work that goes into making veneers reach their full potential in a wooden shop:

1. Material Selection: The process starts with choosing the right finish for the job. Woodworkers look at things like the grain pattern, color, and thickness of the veneer to ensure it fits the rest of the design.
2. Cutting veneers: Specialized tools like veneer saws or rotating cutters are precisely used to cut veneers from logs. How carefully these cuts are made can make a big difference in their appearance.
3. Matching and Sequencing: The veneer sheets must be matched and in the correct order to get a unified look at the end product. This is where the artist's

creativity and care for details come into play.

4. Using glue: Choosing the suitable glue is very important. Many traditional woodworkers use hide glue because it can be used both ways and looks old-fashioned. The coating is put on with glue, and any bubbles or wrinkles are handled.
5. Pressing and clamping: To make a strong bond, putting even pressure all over the veneer is essential. You often need to use vacuum tools or regular clamps during this process.
6. Trimming and sanding: Once the wood is in place, it is cut to fit, and the surface is smoothed. The goal is to have as smooth of a shift as possible between the veneer and the wood underneath.
7. Finishing: The final finish is what makes the item with veneer better. The choice of finish is an art in and of itself, whether it's a clear lacquer to show off the natural beauty of the wood or a fancy hand-rubbed French shine.

Adding veneers to wooden projects gives them a magical look. They let woodworkers combine different kinds of wood to make complicated patterns that would be hard or too expensive to make with solid wood alone. Furniture and artistic pieces have depth and character because of the natural differences in grain and color. Also, veneers are very good at fitting into many styles and times. From the intricate marquetry of the Baroque period to the sleek, minimalist designs of the twenty-first century, veneers have been a flexible and long-lasting way for artists to show their work.

Veneers are more than just a way to save time in the woodshop; they are a canvas for creation and a testament to the skill and passion of artisans. They close the gap between practicality and art by giving woodworkers a way to make long-lasting and beautiful things. So, the next time you enjoy a piece of finely veneered furniture or art, consider the centuries-old skills that made it possible. Veneers are more than just pretty faces; they show you what woodworking is all about.

Book 5: Projects

Introduction

Now that we've made acquaintance with our raw materials, it's time to set sail on the wondrous sea of woodworking projects. In Book 5, we plunge headfirst into the tangible manifestations of a woodworker's creativity. Here, we traverse a spectrum that ranges from the pragmatically functional to the purely aesthetic, where every stroke of the saw and every caress of the chisel is a testament to human ingenuity.

Chapter One

Home Accessories

The classic beauty of wood has never faded, even as steel and glass dominate our modern world. Wood is irreplaceable in our homes due to its unique grains, deep, earthy tones, and warmth. Wood's adaptability is not limited to its use in furniture; it also shines in home accessories, which may elevate the ordinary to the sublime. The realm of wooden home accessories is one where art and science come together in a harmonious union of form and function.

Wooden Platters, the Height of Class:

A wooden tray is one of the most understatedly beautiful pieces of furniture you can add to your home. These trays, crafted from hardwoods like oak, walnut, or maple, are works of art in their own right and a practical necessity. Showcase seasonal fruits in them as a table centerpiece or use them to hold keys and other small items in style by the front door.

Wooden mirrors have a timeless elegance.

Mirrors have a unique role in interior design because they reflect not only our physical selves but also the character of our homes. Mirrors with wooden frames radiate classic elegance. They offer a subtle harmony between the rough and the elegant by bringing nature indoors. Mirrors with wooden frames, whether enormous wall mirrors in the living room or vanity mirrors in the bedroom, can transform a room.

Crafting Beautiful Candlesticks out of Wood:

Candles add a romantic touch and a cozy glow to any space. The atmosphere is elevated to a new level using carved wooden candle holders. Their complex patterns provide hypnotic shadows, setting a mood just right for private meals or quiet reflection. These ornaments are examples of the craftsman's skill at fusing form and function.

Wooden Clocks: A Haven of Calm

Wooden clocks are a throwback to a simpler time when telling time wasn't as easy as checking your phone. Their soothing tones and hypnotic hand movements help us relax at home. These watches, with their wooden cases and faces, represent more than just a means of keeping track of time; they stand as a metaphor for an approach to living that is both deliberate and unhurried.

Wooden shelving's adaptability:

Shelves, both open and closed, made of wood, have been ubiquitous in interior design for centuries. You can display your prized possessions with any shelving, whether a floating, corner, or ladder shelf. Wooden shelves are a great way to add storage space and aesthetic appeal to your home, whether you want to display antique books, plants, or photos.

Customization Using Careful Handwork:

Wooden accents for the home stand out because of how easily they can be customized. Artisans can carve, etch, and inlay exquisite designs, personal monograms, and inspirational sayings into these objects. Besides improving your home's aesthetics, this also strengthens the emotional bond you share with it.

Environmentalism and Timber:

As we move toward a greener tomorrow, wood remains a viable option. Many manufacturers and craftspeople only use wood from sustainably farmed woods, so you may feel good about decorating your home with their wares. The lifespan of wooden objects is another plus; with careful care, they can be handed down through the generations.

Chapter Two

Home Furnishings

Even in this dynamic and ever-evolving world, no place is still like home. We go there to relax, share memories with our loved ones, and be ourselves after a long day. Nothing beats furnishing a house with heirloom-quality pieces made from wood to make a house a home. In this post, we'll look at how completing woodworking projects for home furniture may provide warmth, character, and classic style to our homes for years to come.

Wood's Aesthetics

Wood's natural elegance makes it resistant to passing trends. Its inherent grain patterns, unique textures, and warm colors give it an unrivaled ability to evoke feelings of comfort and fond memory. Whether it's the rich scarlet tones of cherry, the warm amber of oak, or the lovely rusticity of reclaimed wood, every wood species has its unique character. The options mean you may find pieces that complement your personal taste and home decor.

Craftsmanship: Where Art and Science Converge

Wooden furniture stands out because of the skilled craftsmanship that goes into its construction. Skilled artisans infuse their work with not only their expertise but also their enthusiasm. It's often a labor of love, from picking out the perfect piece of wood to the hours spent shaping, sanding, and polishing it. Any knots, nicks, or other imperfections in the wood add to the story and uniqueness of the final product. This kind of individuality is impossible to achieve with mass-produced furniture. It's a gentle reminder that you're not simply buying a table or chair. You're investing in a unique piece of art that carries the spirit of its creator.

Adjusting to Your Specific Preferences and Needs

Wooden furniture is appealing since it can be adapted to the buyer's needs. You can take part in the creative process by placing a commission. You get to choose the species of wood, the stain, the style, and even the dimensions of your custom furniture to perfectly complement your home's aesthetic. To that extent, you can make your furniture unique while fulfilling its practical purpose.

Permanence and Resistance

The durability and resilience of wooden furnishings are well-known. Due to their long lifespan and low replacement costs, they are an environmentally responsible choice. Wood furniture is already relatively eco-friendly due to its natural durability and the fact that it can be made using recycled wood and sustainable forestry practices. In addition to enhancing the beauty of your home, selecting wood will help to make the world a better place.

Soft and toasty

Wood has the remarkable ability to make any space feel more inviting and comfortable. Its intrinsic qualities make it ideal for creating tranquil and restful furniture. Whether it's a handcrafted dining room set around which loved ones gather for meals or a cozy bedroom set that beckons you to relax at the end of the day, wooden furniture brings a sense of warmth and serenity to any home.

Chapter Three

Outdoor Projects

A. Brief Overview of the Importance of Outdoor Woodworking Projects:

Outdoor woodworking projects hold a pivotal role in the world of woodworking, transcending mere functionality to shape and enhance our outdoor living spaces. These projects encompass a wide range of creations, from garden furniture and structures to decking and decorative accents. They bring the craftsmanship and artistic touch of woodworking into the open air, transforming outdoor areas into havens of both utility and beauty.

B. The Intersection of Functionality and Aesthetics in Outdoor Woodworking:

Outdoor woodworking is a unique blend of practicality and aesthetics. Unlike indoor projects, outdoor creations must withstand the challenges posed by nature, including harsh weather conditions, temperature fluctuations, and humidity. This intersection between function and aesthetics means that outdoor woodworkers must carefully balance the structural integrity and durability of their pieces with the visual appeal that contributes to the overall ambiance of an outdoor space.

II. Selecting the Right Wood

A. Discussion of Wood Types Suitable for Outdoor Projects:

The choice of wood is a pivotal decision when embarking on outdoor woodworking projects. Certain wood species are naturally more resistant to decay, insects, and moisture. Woods like cedar, redwood, and teak are popular choices due to their inherent resistance to weather-related issues. Dense hardwoods such as oak, mahogany, and ipe are also favored for their durability. This section provides insights into the characteristics of various wood types, allowing woodworkers to make informed decisions based on the demands of their projects and the environmental factors their creations will face.

B. Considerations for Wood Durability and Resistance to the Elements:

Wood used in outdoor projects is exposed to a spectrum of environmental stressors, including rain, sun, wind, and temperature fluctuations. Understanding the factors that contribute to wood's vulnerability and the mechanisms that lead to deterioration is paramount. This section delves into treatments, finishes, and protective measures that can significantly extend the lifespan of outdoor woodworking projects. It explores topics such as sealing, staining, and applying weather-resistant coatings, helping woodworkers safeguard their creations against the challenges of the elements.

In essence, the introduction sets the stage by highlighting the significance of outdoor woodworking projects, while the discussion on selecting the right wood delves into the practical considerations necessary to create enduring and visually appealing pieces that thrive in outdoor environments. The intersection of functionality and aesthetics remains a guiding principle throughout the woodworking journey, encouraging woodworkers to merge their technical skills with artistic sensibilities to craft pieces that stand the test of time while enriching the outdoor spaces they inhabit.

III. Essential Tools and Safety Measures:

A. List of essential woodworking tools for outdoor projects:

Hand Tools: Include items like chisels, saws, planes, and clamps for precision work.

Power Tools: Essential outdoor woodworking tools may comprise a circular saw, jigsaw, router, and drill for efficient cutting, shaping, and joining.

Measuring and Marking Tools: Quality tape measures, squares, and marking gauges are crucial for precise measurements and layout.

Safety Equipment: Safety glasses, hearing protection, and dust masks safeguard against potential hazards.

B. Emphasizing safety practices and protective gear:

Safety First: Stress the importance of prioritizing safety throughout the woodworking process.

Protective Gear: Explain the necessity of wearing safety goggles, ear protection, and dust masks to prevent injuries.

Work Area Safety: Highlight the significance of maintaining a clean, clutter-free workspace to reduce accidents.

Proper Ventilation: Encourage proper ventilation when working with chemicals like wood sealants or stains.

Tool Safety: Explain how to handle tools safely, emphasizing precautions like keeping hands away from blades and using push sticks.

First Aid Kit: Suggest having a well-equipped first aid kit nearby in case of minor injuries.

Fire Safety: Stress the importance of fire safety, especially when using power tools around flammable materials.

IV. Outdoor Furniture:

A. Crafting wooden benches, chairs, and tables:

Functionality: Explain that outdoor furniture must be designed with comfort and functionality in mind.

Wood Selection: Discuss the suitability of different wood types for furniture, considering factors like weather resistance and aesthetics.

Joinery Techniques: Describe joinery methods such as mortise and tenon or dowels for sturdy furniture construction.

Finishing: Discuss appropriate finishes that protect wood from the elements and enhance its appearance.

B. Design considerations for comfort and style:

Ergonomics: Emphasize the importance of ergonomic design for seating comfort.

Aesthetics: Discuss how design elements like curves, angles, and decorative features can add style to outdoor furniture.

Weather Resistance: Explain how design choices, such as slatted surfaces to facilitate water runoff, can enhance durability.

Customization: Encourage woodworkers to consider customizing designs to fit their preferences and outdoor settings.

C. Treating wood for outdoor use (e.g., sealing, staining):

Wood Protection: Explain the necessity of treating outdoor wood to protect it from moisture, UV rays, and insects.

Sealing: Discuss the use of sealants to create a protective barrier against moisture.

Staining: Describe how wood staining not only protects but also enhances the appearance of outdoor furniture.

Maintenance: Stress the importance of regular maintenance, including resealing or restaining as needed to prolong the life of the furniture.

Environmentally Friendly Options: Mention eco-friendly wood treatments for those concerned about environmental impact.

VI. Decking and Flooring:

A. Constructing Wooden Decks and Patios:

Constructing wooden decks and patios is a pivotal aspect of outdoor woodworking, allowing individuals to transform their outdoor spaces into functional and inviting areas. Decks and patios serve as extensions of indoor living, providing spaces for relaxation, entertainment, and social gatherings. This section delves into the step-by-step process of building these platforms using wood, from preparing the ground and creating a solid foundation to attaching joists and decking boards. It emphasizes the importance of structural integrity, proper fastening techniques, and ensuring that the deck or patio is level and stable. By providing clear instructions, safety tips, and guidance on choosing suitable wood, this section equips woodworkers with the skills needed to create sturdy, long-lasting outdoor platforms.

B. Discussing Deck Design, Layout, and Elevation:

The design of a deck or patio significantly impacts its functionality and aesthetic appeal. This subsection delves into the art of deck design, covering considerations such as layout, size, shape, and elevation. It emphasizes how the design should harmonize with the surrounding landscape, complementing the architectural style of the home while optimizing space usage. Discussions on elevation guide woodworkers in creating multi-level decks that accommodate different activities and create visual interest. Additionally, the section underscores the importance of planning for railings, stairs, and access points, enhancing both safety and accessibility.

C. Finishing Options for Outdoor Flooring:

The choice of finishing options for outdoor flooring plays a vital role in the durability and appearance of decks and patios. This part of the chapter explores various finishing techniques that protect the wood from weathering, UV exposure, and moisture damage. It covers staining, sealing, and painting, detailing the pros and cons of each approach. The discussion also includes advice on selecting finishes that complement the overall design of the outdoor space. By providing insights into finishing methods, this section empowers woodworkers to enhance the beauty of their creations while extending their lifespan in the face of outdoor elements.

VII. Outdoor Storage Solutions:

A. Building Sheds, Storage Benches, and Cabinets:

Outdoor storage solutions are essential for maintaining a clutter-free and organized outdoor area. This subsection focuses on constructing functional and visually appealing storage structures, such as sheds, storage benches, and cabinets. It guides woodworkers through the construction process, including framing, siding, roofing, and creating storage compartments. Emphasis is placed on choosing durable materials that can withstand exposure to the elements and providing detailed instructions to ensure the proper assembly of these structures

B. Maximizing Space While Maintaining a Neat Appearance:

Effectively utilizing outdoor storage solutions involves a balance between maximizing storage capacity and maintaining an attractive outdoor environment. This part of the chapter explores strategies for optimizing storage space through creative design, adjustable shelving, and innovative storage solutions. It emphasizes the importance of integrating these structures seamlessly into the landscape to preserve the aesthetic appeal of the outdoor space. By guiding woodworkers on creating storage solutions that blend functionality and aesthetics, this section helps them transform their outdoor areas into well-organized, tidy, and inviting spaces.

VIII. Decorative Accents:

A. Crafting Wooden Planters, Birdhouses, and Decorative Screens:

In the realm of outdoor woodworking, crafting decorative accents goes beyond mere functionality and delves into the realm of artistic expression. This section emphasizes the creation of wooden planters, birdhouses, and decorative screens to add aesthetic value to outdoor spaces. Wooden planters can be crafted in various shapes and sizes, allowing for a blend of nature and craftsmanship. Birdhouses provide shelter for local avian inhabitants while also serving as charming ornaments. Decorative screens, intricately designed and crafted, can offer both privacy and a sense of elegance to outdoor areas.

B. Enhancing Outdoor Spaces with Artistic Woodworking Elements:

Outdoor spaces become truly captivating when artistic woodworking elements are introduced. By carefully selecting and placing these elements, woodworkers can transform mundane areas into captivating havens. This could include hand-carved wooden sculptures, intricate lattice work, or even wooden mosaics. Each piece is an opportunity to showcase craftsmanship and creativity, harmonizing the natural surroundings with human-made beauty. These elements not only enhance visual appeal but also contribute to the overall atmosphere of tranquility and inspiration that outdoor spaces can provide.

IX. Maintenance and Weatherproofing:

A. Strategies for Preserving the Longevity of Outdoor Woodwork:

While the creation of outdoor woodworking projects is an art in itself, their preservation over time is equally important. This section delves into strategies for ensuring the longevity of these pieces. It covers aspects such as selecting the right type of wood that is naturally resistant to weather and pests, as well as treating the wood with appropriate finishes and sealants. Proper wood treatment not only enhances the appearance but also shields against the harmful effects of moisture, UV rays, and temperature changes.

B. Regular Maintenance Routines to Protect Against Weathering:

Woodwork exposed to the elements requires consistent care to counteract the effects of weathering. This part of the "Woodworking Bible" emphasizes the significance of regular maintenance routines. This could include practices like inspecting for cracks or signs of deterioration, cleaning the wood surfaces, and reapplying protective finishes as needed. By establishing a routine maintenance schedule, woodworkers can ensure that their outdoor creations continue to stand strong against the challenges of time and weather, preserving their beauty and functionality for years to come.

Chapter Four

Workshop Projects

A. Definition and Significance of Workshop Projects:

Workshop projects within the context of the Woodworking Bible refer to hands-on crafting endeavors that allow individuals to create functional and artistic pieces using woodworking techniques. These projects span a wide range of complexity, from simple beginner-friendly tasks to intricate and advanced designs. The significance of workshop projects lies in their ability to bridge the gap between theory and practice. They offer woodworkers the opportunity to apply the principles and skills they learn from the Woodworking Bible's guidance in a real-world setting, fostering a deeper understanding of the craft.

B. The Role of Workshop Projects in Woodworking Education:

Workshop projects play a pivotal role in woodworking education as they serve as tangible learning experiences. While the Woodworking Bible imparts knowledge about tools, techniques, and design, workshop projects provide a practical outlet for this knowledge. They allow woodworkers to develop tactile skills, problem-solving abilities, and a keen sense of precision. Moreover, workshop projects cater to different skill levels, providing a natural progression from novice to expert. These projects encourage individuals to engage in continuous learning and improvement, nurturing a sense of accomplishment and confidence in their woodworking journey.

II. Types of Workshop Projects

A. Small-scale Projects for Beginners

1. Examples: Simple Shelves, Tool Organizers

Small-scale workshop projects are designed to introduce beginners to woodworking fundamentals. These projects might include crafting basic items like simple shelves or tool organizers. These tasks focus on fundamental skills such as measuring, cutting, and assembly. Creating a small shelf, for instance, involves understanding measurements, making accurate cuts, and joining pieces securely. Similarly, crafting a tool organizer requires planning tool layouts and constructing compartments for efficient storage. These projects provide a low-pressure environment for beginners to build foundational skills before tackling more complex endeavors.

2. Importance of Starting with Small Projects:

Starting with small projects is crucial for several reasons. Firstly, they allow beginners to grasp essential woodworking techniques without feeling overwhelmed. As novices gain experience and confidence through these small successes, they're more likely to advance to larger, more intricate projects. Additionally, small projects often require a limited set of tools and materials, making them budget-friendly and accessible for those just beginning their woodworking journey. As beginners complete these projects, they lay the groundwork for enhanced problem-solving skills, patience, and attention to detail traits that will serve them well as they progress to more ambitious creations.

B. Intermediate-level projects

Examples: tables, chairs, cabinets: Intermediate-level workshop projects in the

Woodworking Bible encompass a diverse range of furniture pieces. Tables, for instance, are excellent projects to transition from beginner to intermediate levels. Crafting a table involves skills such as creating flat, level surfaces, constructing sturdy legs, and ensuring proper alignment. It also introduces woodworking enthusiasts to considerations like sizing and proportionality.

Chairs are another intermediate project, requiring a deeper understanding of ergonomics and comfort. Crafting chair components, such as the backrest and seat, demands precise measurements and angles. Intermediate woodworkers learn how to create pieces that are not just functional but also comfortable and aesthetically pleasing.

Cabinets, the third example, delve into the realm of storage solutions. These projects involve advanced concepts such as designing efficient layouts, crafting intricate joinery for doors and drawers, and ensuring stability. Intermediate woodworkers gain valuable insights into spatial planning and organization.

Developing more advanced skills: Intermediate-level projects serve as a bridge between foundational skills and advanced craftsmanship. Woodworkers at this stage begin to refine their techniques, focusing on accuracy, precision, and aesthetics. They develop a deeper understanding of wood grain, selection, and joinery methods. Additionally, these projects encourage woodworkers to experiment with more complex designs and incorporate decorative elements, expanding their creative horizons.

C. Advanced and intricate projects

Examples: intricate joinery, detailed carvings: Advanced and intricate workshop projects exemplify the pinnacle of woodworking expertise. These projects often involve intricate joinery techniques, such as dovetails, mortise and tenon, and finger joints. Mastery of these techniques is essential for achieving both structural integrity and visual appeal in fine woodworking.

Detailed carvings represent another facet of advanced projects. Woodworkers may tackle intricate relief carvings, in which they sculpt intricate patterns and designs into the wood. This demands a keen eye for detail, as well as the ability to manipulate carving tools with precision. These projects often result in heirloom-quality pieces that showcase the woodworker's artistic prowess.

Pushing the boundaries of woodworking expertise: Advanced and intricate projects challenge woodworkers to push the boundaries of their skills and creativity. They require meticulous planning and execution, often involving complex assemblies and precise measurements. Woodworkers at this stage must also possess an in-depth understanding of wood characteristics, as different woods behave uniquely during carving and joinery processes.

These projects offer an opportunity for woodworkers to express their individual style and creativity. They may incorporate custom inlays, marquetry, or other embellishments that elevate the piece to a work of art. While challenging, advanced and intricate projects are immensely rewarding, showcasing the culmination of a woodworker's dedication and mastery of the craft.

III. Tools and Materials for Workshop Projects:

A. Overview of essential woodworking tools

Hand tools: Hand tools form the foundation of any woodworking toolkit. They include essentials like chisels, hand planes, saws, hammers, and measuring tools. Chisels are used for precise carving and shaping, hand planes for smoothing surfaces, saws for cutting, hammers for driving in joinery, and measuring tools for accuracy. Understanding the use and maintenance of these hand tools is crucial for achieving craftsmanship in woodworking.

Power tools: Power tools complement hand tools, offering efficiency and precision. The Woodworking Bible introduces woodworkers to power tools such as table saws, band saws, routers, and drills. These tools enable woodworkers to tackle larger projects and achieve consistent results. Safety measures, including proper handling and safety gear, are emphasized when using power tools.

B. Selection of appropriate wood species

Selecting the right wood species is a critical aspect of woodworking. The Woodworking Bible educates woodworkers on different types of wood, including hardwoods like oak, maple, and cherry, and softwoods like pine and cedar. Each wood species has unique characteristics in terms of grain pattern, hardness, and color, affecting both the appearance and durability of the final project.

Understanding wood properties is essential for making informed decisions regarding project suitability and aesthetics. For instance, some woods are better suited for intricate carving due to their fine grain, while others are chosen for their durability in outdoor applications. The Woodworking Bible provides guidance on choosing the appropriate wood species to match the project's requirements and desired outcome.

C. Understanding different finishes and hardware

Achieving a professional finish is a crucial aspect of woodworking. The Woodworking Bible covers various finishing techniques, including staining, varnishing, and applying protective coatings like polyurethane. It explains how different finishes can enhance the wood's natural beauty and protect it from environmental factors.

IV. Planning and Design

A. Importance of Detailed Planning:

In woodworking, detailed planning is the cornerstone of a successful project. Before you even pick up a piece of wood, taking the time to thoroughly plan your project can save you countless hours of frustration and help you achieve the desired outcome. This involves visualizing the end product, understanding its purpose, and determining the specific requirements, such as dimensions, materials, and design elements. A well-planned project minimizes the chances of mistakes and ensures that you have a clear roadmap to follow.

B. Creating Project Blueprints and Sketches:

Blueprints and sketches serve as your project's blueprint, guiding you through each step of the construction process. These visual representations allow you to see the project from multiple angles, make necessary adjustments, and visualize how different components will come together. You can use drafting tools or even software to create precise drawings that outline measurements, joinery methods, and overall design. These blueprints become invaluable references as you move forward with your project.

C. Measuring, Cutting, and Shaping Wood:

Accurate measurements are the foundation of woodworking. Taking precise measurements ensures that your project components fit together seamlessly. Once you have your measurements, you can proceed with cutting and shaping the wood. Depending on your project, this might involve using hand tools like saws, chisels, and planes, or power tools such as table saws and routers. Proper technique and attention to detail during this phase contribute to the overall quality of your finished piece.

D. Ensuring Safety Precautions During the Planning Phase:

Safety should never be overlooked during any phase of woodworking, including planning. Before you start working on your project, consider the tools and materials you'll be using, and assess potential risks. Make sure you're familiar with the correct usage of tools, wear appropriate safety gear such as safety glasses and ear protection, and work in a well-ventilated area if you're using finishes or adhesives. By incorporating safety into your planning, you're establishing a mindset of responsible woodworking from the outset.

V. Building Workshop Projects

A. Step-by-Step Construction Process:

Following a systematic step-by-step approach is key to managing the complexity of woodworking projects. Begin with the foundational elements and progress methodically through each stage. This might involve creating sub-assemblies before joining them together, ensuring that each part is accurately crafted and fitted. Breaking down the process into manageable steps allows you to focus on one task at a time and prevents overwhelm.

B. Assembling and Joining Techniques:

Joinery is a fundamental aspect of woodworking. Different projects require different joining techniques, such as dovetails, mortise and tenon, biscuits, and dowels. Understanding the strengths and limitations of each technique empowers you to choose the most suitable one for your project. Precise execution of joinery ensures the stability and longevity of your finished piece.

C. Tips for Achieving Precision and Accuracy:

Precision and accuracy are marks of a skilled woodworker. Use sharp and well-maintained tools to achieve clean cuts and accurate measurements. Take your time during each step, double-checking measurements before cutting, and using guides or jigs to ensure consistent results. Remember, a small error early in the process can compound as you progress, so attention to detail is paramount.

D. Troubleshooting Common Issues:

Woodworking rarely goes entirely according to plan, and that's where troubleshooting comes in. From minor misalignments to unexpected challenges, knowing how to identify and address issues as they arise is crucial. This might involve using techniques to adjust fit, employing filler or patches, or even rethinking certain design elements. Developing problem-solving skills is a natural part of becoming a proficient woodworker.

VI. Finishing and Detailing

A. Applying Wood Finishes: Applying wood finishes is a crucial step in workshop projects as it not only enhances the appearance of the wood but also protects it from moisture, UV rays, and wear. There are various types of finishes to choose from, including oils, varnishes, stains, and paints. Choosing the right finish depends on the intended use of the project and the desired aesthetic. The application process involves sanding the surface, applying the finish evenly, and allowing it to dry properly between coats. This step brings out the wood's natural beauty and adds depth to the project.

B. Sanding and Smoothing Surfaces: Sanding plays a vital role in achieving a professional and polished look for your workshop projects. It helps to remove any rough edges, uneven surfaces, or tool marks. Starting with a coarse grit and progressively moving to finer grits, sanding creates a smooth and even surface for the finish to adhere to. Proper sanding also ensures that there are no splinters or sharp edges that could potentially harm users of the finished project.

C. Adding Decorative Elements: Adding decorative elements to your workshop projects can turn them into personalized works of art. This can include carving intricate designs, inlaying contrasting wood pieces, or using woodburning techniques to create patterns. These elements not only showcase your creativity but also make your project stand out and become a unique expression of your woodworking skills.

D. Final Quality Checks: Before declaring a project complete, it's essential to conduct thorough quality checks. Inspect for any flaws, gaps, or imperfections that might have been missed during construction or finishing. Verify that all joints are secure and that the project meets the intended design specifications. Address any issues and make necessary adjustments to ensure that your workshop project is of the highest quality before presenting or using it.

VII. Workshop Projects in Skill Development

A. How Workshop Projects Contribute to Skill Progression: Workshop projects provide a structured and practical way to develop woodworking skills. As you progress from simpler projects to more complex ones, you encounter a variety of techniques and challenges. Each project introduces new skills, such as precise measuring, joinery methods, and intricate detailing. The cumulative experience gained from these projects gradually builds your skill set, allowing you to tackle increasingly intricate and ambitious creations.

B. Learning from Mistakes and Refining Techniques: Workshop projects are excellent learning opportunities, often involving trial and error. Mistakes become valuable lessons that enhance your problem-solving skills and deepen your understanding of woodworking principles. With each project, you refine your techniques, finding more efficient ways to handle tasks and improving your ability to troubleshoot unexpected issues.

C. Building Confidence in Woodworking Abilities: The completion of workshop projects contributes to a sense of accomplishment and boosts your confidence as a woodworker. As you overcome challenges and witness your progress, you develop a belief in your abilities. This confidence not only benefits your woodworking endeavors but can also extend to other aspects of your life, fostering a growth mindset and a willingness to take on new challenges.

VIII. Showcasing Workshop Projects

A. Importance of Displaying and Sharing Completed Projects: Displaying and sharing completed workshop projects is essential for several reasons. It allows you to celebrate your achievements, receive feedback from others, and inspire fellow woodworkers. When projects are on display, they serve as a reminder of your accomplishments and encourage you to continue refining your skills. Additionally, sharing your work can lead to opportunities for collaboration, learning, and networking within the woodworking community.

B. Building a Woodworking Portfolio: Creating a woodworking portfolio helps you document your progression as a woodworker. Include high-quality photographs of your projects, along with descriptions of the techniques and challenges you tackled. A portfolio not only showcases your skills to potential clients or employers but also serves as a personal record of your growth and creative journey.

C. Participating in Woodworking Communities and Exhibitions: Joining woodworking communities and participating in exhibitions allows you to connect with fellow enthusiasts, learn from experienced woodworkers, and gain exposure for your work.

Exhibiting your projects in woodworking shows or online platforms provides an opportunity to receive constructive feedback, build your reputation, and even attract potential buyers if you're interested in turning your hobby into a business.

Conclusion

In the realm of woodworking, books 4 and 5 are the foundation and the manifestation. We've explored the very essence of the craft, from the diverse world of woods to the tangible beauty of woodworking projects. As you embark on your woodworking odyssey, may you find inspiration in the grain of the wood, and may your creations forever echo with the touch of your craftsmanship. Remember, every piece of wood holds a story, and as a woodworker, you have the privilege of shaping its narrative. Happy woodworking!